Dealing with Delinquents

I0127699

W. L. Herbert and F. V. Jarvis

Routledge
Taylor & Francis Group

First published in 1961
by Methuen & Co. Ltd

This edition first published in 2025 by Routledge
4 Park Square, Milton Park, Abingdon, Oxon, OX14 4RN

and by Routledge
605 Third Avenue, New York, NY 10017

Routledge is an imprint of the Taylor & Francis Group, an informa business

© 1961 W. L. Herbert and F. V. Jarvis

Publisher's Note
The publisher has gone to great lengths to ensure the quality of this reprint but points out that some imperfections in the original copies may be apparent.

Disclaimer
The publisher has made every effort to trace copyright holders and welcomes correspondence from those they have been unable to contact.

A Library of Congress record exists under LCCN: 64039343

ISBN: 978-1-032-90562-4 (hbk)
ISBN: 978-1-003-55859-0 (ebk)
ISBN: 978-1-032-90570-9 (pbk)

Book DOI 10.4324/9781003558590

Dealing
with Delinquents

by
W. L. HERBERT
and F. V. JARVIS

LONDON

METHUEN & CO LTD

36 ESSEX STREET · WC2

First published 1961
© *1961 by W. L. Herbert and F. V. Jarvis*
Printed and bound in Great Britain by
Cox & Wyman Ltd, Fakenham
CATALOGUE NO. 2/6446/1

Contents

CONTENTS

Acknowledgments

Many people have helped the authors in the writing of this book. They are particularly grateful to Dr Howard Jones and to Jack and Christine Porter, who read the manuscript at various stages and offered many useful criticisms and suggestions. They also appreciate the kindness of Mr H. A. Prins and Mr A. B. R. MacGillivray in reading the completed typescript. None of these is in any way identified with the ideas expressed, for which the authors alone take responsibility. Finally they would like to thank Miss Sandra Farmer for her help with the clerical work.

Acknowledgements

Introduction

Our purpose in this book is to show how some delinquents may be treated in their own home environment in such a way that they are able to conform to standards of behaviour which the community can accept. Not all delinquency can be so treated, nor all delinquents, and the treatment of the delinquent in the open is not proposed as a substitute for institutional treatment. These two methods exist side by side. One may support and supplement the other, but does not replace it. However, we are not here concerned with institutional treatment.

We offer no general 'cure' for delinquency. Our argument simply is that with the right person at the right time and in the right place 'treatment by social worker' can be effective.

We have not aimed at a comprehensive study of the causes of delinquency. This has been attempted by others, but as yet there is no generally accepted theory of causation. We are concerned with causes in this book only in so far as they can be linked up with practical methods of treatment.

The techniques we offer have partly developed empirically from the experiences of social workers – particularly probation officers – over the past fifty years. This process has been one of 'doing it badly' and thereby painfully learning to 'do it better'. In addition, we have drawn eclectically upon ideas arising from the inquiries of others, where these strengthen and clarify practical experience. Thus some sort of rudimentary theoretical framework is provided. In a broad sense the book represents the application to delinquency of the methods outlined in *A Modern Approach to Marriage Counselling*.[1]

The work of dealing with delinquents in the open is not a simple matter. It requires, ideally, both training and experience. It is to assist in this training and to give depth to this experience that our book has primarily been written. We believe it will be of value to the social work student and also to the practising social worker. Particularly do we hope that it will confirm in the latter a belief that he possesses a consistent and effective technique which he can pass on to others. We hope too that what we have written will be of assistance to teachers – especially teachers in training – and to clergy in their pastoral work. Finally, the book may help the responsible citizen in his understanding of some of the problems of delinquency.

I

The Social Worker and The Delinquent

What is a delinquent? People use the word to convey a variety of meanings. For some a delinquent is one who has offended against the criminal law. For others, he is a person who has broken only minor laws – those which do not disturb the public conscience too much. Yet other people use the word purely for young offenders, neglecting even to prefix it with the word 'juvenile'.

In this book we include in the term 'delinquent' not only those who have actually broken laws – minor or otherwise – but those who are likely to do so. In our sense, a delinquent is a person, of whatever age, whose attitude to other individuals, to the community, to lawful authority, is such that it may lead him into breaking the law, if it has not already done so. Persistent truants, or children beyond the control of their parents – whether or not it is the parents' fault – would come within this definition.

It could be said that some breaches of the law represent only minor acts of omission, or merely technical offences, and are not really delinquent. Trivial traffic offences or breaches of shop bye-laws would be examples of these. We must agree that the person who commits an isolated offence of this sort is not our concern in this book. Persistent transgression of even minor regulations, however, may sometimes indicate an attitude to society verging on the delinquent.

Clearly, the total of delinquents covered by our definition is greater than that which is shown by the criminal statistics. Criminal statistics are concerned only with persons actually dealt with by a court. Our definition includes not only those who, while likely to commit an offence, have not yet done so, but also delinquents whose offences have not been reported or, if reported, have not been detected. In addition, it includes delinquents whose offences are detected but who are dealt with in some way other than by a court. The actual numbers in these categories are not known, but criminologists are satisfied that they far exceed those that figure in the criminal statistics.

So much for what a delinquent is, in so far as this book is concerned. Next, how can he be dealt with? Human society has never found it easy to deal with its delinquents. It has developed a very wide range of remedies and it is interesting to review some of these.

There are, firstly, the milder remedies: persuasion, exhortation, admonition, threat, promise, appeal to self-interest or the interests of others. All these belong to the armoury of parents and pedagogues, and most people have both used and suffered them.

If the delinquent deviation appears to be within the range of mental illness, society, through the medical profession, tries such treatments as psychotherapy, group therapy, psycho-analysis, drugs, electric shock therapy, or brain surgery.

Removal of the delinquent person from his present environment is a common remedy. It is a form of treatment which is primarily reformative in purpose, and in this it differs from imprisonment which has also a punitive intent. It does, however, shade gradually into punishment. Schools for maladjusted children, homes for neglectful mothers, inebriates' retreats, homes and hostels of different kinds, approved schools – there are many alternatives of this kind.

From these we can logically move to punishment proper, which is intended to have a direct retributive or deterrent effect upon the offender and an indirect deterrent effect upon others. There is, for instance, corporal punishment. Once widely used for all ages and both sexes, it is at present reserved mainly for boys at school. The range of corporal punishment extends from smacking and caning to flogging – now reserved in this country for the punishment of assaults on prison officers – and thence to physical torture which, happily, we no longer use, but which is common enough in some other countries, for political rather than criminal offenders.

Monetary penalties are widely used. They range from the minor deprivations imposed by parents, to the imposition of fines and the ordering of restitution by the courts. The sequestration and confiscation of property, although still practised in totalitarian states, is a matter of history in this country.

Imprisonment is perhaps the most characteristic form of punishment in modern society. It may be accompanied by varying degrees of physical discomfort and combined with varying efforts at reformation. Finally, there is removal from society altogether – by banishment or transportation, in the old days, or by the supreme sanction of death.

It would be wrong to imagine that society has always been motivated by the relatively benign purposes of reformation or deterrence in its treatment of the delinquent. Retribution has played its part, and is still an element in the penal code of this country. It would be interesting to consider the fluctuating emphasis on retribution, deterrence and reformation in the recent penological history of our society. For our present purpose, it is sufficient to notice that in the permissive atmosphere of the modern community there is considerable tolerance of the delinquent and a widespread desire to reform him without harming him and his dependants.

Somewhere among the welter of remedies is the treatment of the offender 'in the open'. In the open means in the delinquent's own home environment and not in an institution. The treatment does not involve punishment as such. With young delinquents it could in theory be carried out by parent or guardian, but in fact most parents and guardians of delinquents are incapable of doing it unless they are given some help. Treatment of delinquents in the open, as we intend it to be understood, is usually carried out by social workers or by people with the outlook of social workers. 'Treatment by social worker' is the best descriptive phrase for it.

Treatment by social worker is a possibility only in a society which is secure enough to have a reasonable tolerance of delinquents, which is not over-authoritarian and which sees an intrinsic value in the individual. The method has attractions other than clemency and efficacy: it is cheap. In 1958, for example, the Probation Service dealt successfully with 74 per cent of the delinquents placed on probation at an average cost of something in the region of ten shillings per head per week. By contrast, treatment in Borstals and prisons cost something like twelve pounds and eight pounds per head per week respectively. In addition, a delinquent on probation and in employment is able not only to make a contribution to the economy of the community but also to maintain his dependants and himself by his own efforts. This he is unable to do if he is in an institution. It is not suggested that such treatment is necessarily more efficacious than institutional treatment. We are merely indicating its economic advantages from the point of view of the community.

What kinds of social workers are in touch with delinquents and may be expected to deal with them in the open? We have already mentioned the Probation Service, and indeed probation officers are the community's principal agents in this type of treatment. Originally, as police court missionaries, they were employed by a voluntary body – the Church of England Temperance Society – and their early work was mainly with drunkards and their families. Today, they form a locally-controlled state service about fifteen hundred strong and are available to every criminal court in the country. Their main duty is to 'advise, assist and befriend' offenders placed on probation by the courts. Any offender, whatever his age, whatever his previous history, and whatever his offence – unless it be one of the very few which carries a fixed statutory penalty as does murder or treason – may be placed under their supervision. They also have a duty, when asked by the court, to supply background reports on offenders. In addition, they provide after-care supervision for a wide range of offenders released from institutions. It will be apparent from this that their contact with delinquents is wide and varied.[2]

No other social workers have anything like the same professional opportunities for attempting treatment in the open, but many people, both professional and lay, meet delinquents and try to help them. Those who work in child guidance clinics do so, for example. The police in a different way try to help, and in a few areas allocate officers, known as police liaison officers, to work with youthful delinquents who have been officially cautioned but have not been brought before the court. Over and above this, the police may be expected generally to give advice and help to offenders who seem to want to keep out of further trouble. This is particularly true of the women police, whose functions include a strong element of social work.

Child care officers of the local authority Children's Departments are principally concerned with children deprived of a normal home life through neglect, cruelty, illness, or other reasons and who are in the care of the local authority. Some of these children are delinquent, or incipiently delinquent, and their reform is very much a concern of the child care officer.

Education welfare officers are well aware that truancy is often associated with delinquency. They too are often dealing with delinquents before they have reached the court and many work with individual children in the hope of effecting a 'cure'. Moral welfare workers know that among their unmarried mothers there are delinquents in the wider sense, if not in the narrower sense of law-breakers. While giving the necessary practical help, they often attempt also to assist the girl towards a happier and more satisfactory relationship with her family and with society.

School-teachers and club-leaders inevitably meet a proportion of delinquents among their charges. Theirs is a particularly difficult task, for, while wishing to help the individual wrong-doer, they must at the same time bear in mind the needs and interests of the majority for whom they are responsible. Yet teachers especially can do much towards the treatment of delinquency in the open, not least because they often see it in its early stage. We consider this to be so important that we have devoted a special chapter to it.

Hostel wardens, health visitors, N.S.P.C.C. inspectors, medical practitioners, clergy, welfare workers of all kinds – the range of well-disposed people who meet and wish to help delinquents is wide. Despite differing religious and philosophical orientations, they are alike in their object : they all hope by personal contact with the delinquent to influence his behaviour. On the question of actual technique, however, there is little accord, simply because a coherent body of treatment principles has yet to be accepted. The old-fashioned didactic enunciation of moral precepts has been found insufficient in many ways, but there is varied opinion and some hesitation as to what is to take its place.

It might be thought that the Probation Service, with is unrivalled experience ranging over some eighty years, would by now have produced a set of generally accepted treatment principles. Certainly, it is closer to this now than it ever has been. The actual mechanics of the method used are well established. They involve a series of regular meetings between probation officer and delinquent over a considerable period, at the probation office or the delinquent's home, or both. These meetings are initiated and if necessary enforced by the probation officer. They are combined with a contact with the delinquent's family, varying in intensity for individual cases. Encouragement, friendship, advice, admonition, exhortation, direction and warning may all be part of

B

the relationship between the probation officer and his probationer. The emphasis is shifted by the probation officer as the case seems to require. This work is often accompanied by efforts to alter the delinquent's environment for the better. The contact with the family frequently has this end in view, and the probation officer may also be concerned with the probationer's employment, school, companions and leisure interests.

It cannot be denied that this method is often successful. It is only comparatively recently, however, that probation officers, along with other social workers, have looked self-consciously at what they are doing. How and why the method works, and what the basic principles are which underlie it, will become apparent as we proceed.

II

Theories About Delinquency

The social worker's approach to the problem of delinquency has tended to be an empirical one. He has done what seemed right to him in the light of his own intuition. Where he has changed his techniques it has been as a result of his individual experience rather than a response to the promptings of a new theory. Not until comparatively recently has there been any real attempt to relate the social worker's efforts to any general premise. Even today he is attracted more to theories about treatment than to theories of causation. This is not only because basic causes have seemed hitherto to have little practical relevance to his day-to-day work. It is also because, while many factors contributing to delinquency are known, a viable general theory of causation has not been available.

Our immediate concern in this book is not with the causes of crime but with its treatment. We want to help social workers in *dealing* with delinquents in the open. It may be useful, however, if, at the outset, we mention briefly some of the theories about delinquency which are relevant to our approach. It is particularly for students that we do this, and the general reader may prefer to pass on to the next chapter.

Professor Sir Cyril Burt was possibly the first writer in this country to suggest a scientific causation for juvenile delinquency. In his work on the subject, first published in 1925,[3] he sets out the results of his careful research. 'Is there,' he asks, 'any all-pervading principle, whether of causation or treatment?' His answer lies in what he called 'multiple determination'. 'Crime,' he says, 'springs from a multiplicity of alternative and converging influences.' Referring to his statistics, he says that 'In all, more that 170 distinct conditions have been encountered, every one of them conducive to childish misconduct.' He discovered, in addition, that these types of conditions were not peculiar to delinquents: they were observed in non-delinquents also. Consequently, he goes on, 'It must therefore as a rule be either the number of factors or the peculiar combination of them that renders delinquency a probable result.' He groups his multitude of causal influences into hereditary, environmental, physical, and psychological conditions. His conclusion, hedged about with such words as 'tentative', 'provisional', and 'first approximation', is that an intensive study of the child and his conditions may afford 'some warrantable guide for discreet prognostications'.

Social workers have found his book of immense interest and profit over the years. Burt diverted their attention from the wickedness and moral depravity of delinquency in general and directed it to the need to understand each individual offender and his circumstances. In this his influence has been invaluable. So far as his 'multiple determination' theory is concerned, it may be scientific, but it is certainly daunting. The social worker in contemplating the '170 distinct conditions' could be excused for feeling himself not much nearer to his real need—a simple and clearly-stated technique for dealing with delinquent conduct.

William Healy and Augusta Bronner, two Americans,

published in 1936 a work called *New Light on Delinquency and its Treatment*,[4] one of a series of books based upon careful research. Healy and Bronner saw delinquency as representing 'the expression of desires and urges which otherwise are unsatisfied'. 'It is,' they said, 'just such a response to inner drives and outer stimuli as any other kind of conduct.' The social worker noted that sin and wickedness and free-will were not in the centre of the picture. The authors merely said that 'the barrier which we call the conscience or the super-ego is universally found, but in different individuals plays various and partial roles in determining and motivating behaviour'. Delinquency for them was a result of 'frustrations of fundamental urges, desires and wishes which belong to the normal stream of life's activities.' Chief among these urges, desires and wishes were the need for affectionate, secure human relationships, and for the recognition of personality; opportunity for the realization of social adequacy by satisfactory accomplishment; the need for independence, for new experiences, and for outlets and possessions. It was the blocking of one or more of these which led to delinquency.

But how did they become blocked? 'Unsatisfying human relationships form obstructions to the flow of normal urges, desires and wishes in the channels of socially acceptable activities' stated Healy and Bronner. The 'unsatisfying relationships', they said, were 'mainly within the family group, where the attitudes and behaviour of parents and others are influenced by their own personal dissatisfactions'. Here we have it for the first time: a major causal factor in delinquency, according to Healy and Bronner, is failure to make successful or satisfying relationships within the family.

21

Let us now look at what has been designated the ecological school. Clifford Shaw and Henry McKay in the United States showed that crime in a city (they were referring to American cities of the 1920's and 1930's) seemed to be more intense in the centre than at the periphery.[5] This had importance if only because it led inquirers to consider the sort of people who lived at the centre. In the cities studied by Shaw and McKay, the centre was the oldest part and was usually a slum which housed the poorer, the less successful and the less socially orientated members of the community. Modern re-housing has often dispersed these elements around the periphery of the city.

However, the ecological approach still has relevance in that its protagonists have clearly shown that some districts are more productive of delinquency than others.[6], [7], [8] The general impression conveyed by these writers is that if delinquency is tied up with social environment, then its elimination must await changes in that environment. Clifford Shaw seems to believe that this must be the principal method of treatment. In this book, however, we are dealing with individuals as social workers meet them here and now, so that we are not concerned directly with the possible results of large-scale environmental changes. We can only observe that peripheral housing estates seem in our experience just as 'delinquency producing' as the old city slum centres.

Where the proponents of the ecological school turn to the examination of individual delinquents and their families, their work has greater relevance for us. Mays, for instance, divides his delinquents into 'environmental delinquents' whom he identifies with the occasional law-breakers, and 'emotionally maladjusted criminals' who,

22

he believes, are the chronic law-breakers. Morris, too distinguishes between 'psychiatric delinquency', which he sees as related to serious emotional disturbances in the family or to mental ill-health, and 'social delinquency' which, he says, is related to the cultural milieu of the delinquent. But he goes on to state that in his view, legally-defined delinquency at least is a social character-istic of the working-classes in general and the family of the unskilled labourer in particular.

Ferguson also found that delinquency was more fre-quent among the children of unskilled workers. This does not mean that delinquency is necessarily associated with poverty, for the present-day unskilled labourer is not always poor and the working-class in general is no longer necessarily identified with the lower income groups. The important truth seems to be that the way the individual delinquent is brought up is greatly signifi-cant. Morris makes this point. Following Cohen, an American writer,[9] he sees the working-class family as deficient in inculcating such attributes as self-control and restraint, and as failing to provide a harmonious family life and outlets for leisure interests. W. J. H. Sprott,[10] another of the ecological school, has listed the characteristics of the family lives of people living in a delinquency area. Healy and Bronner also concede that bad neighbourhoods, bad associates and poor recrea-tional facilities are destructive influences; but they point out that even in these conditions a large number are nevertheless not delinquent. This is a fundamental point.

Louis Bovet, in his report to the World Health Organization in 1951,[11] stated that insecurity which gave rise to anxiety was at the root of most delinquency. Anxiety he defined in a special sense as 'fear without an object'. His view was that 'imperfect adaptation' to the necessities of the external social world resulted in objective or subjective insecurity. This 'imperfect adaptation', he said, might arise from physical illness or infirmity; from unfavourable social conditions, such as bad housing and bad companions; from wars, revolutions and industrial upheavals; or from faulty emotional development. Any of these could engender insecurity from which anxiety arose. Aggression or crime were forms of relief from this anxiety.

This theory appears to take in everything as completely and rather more neatly than that of Burt. Yet as it stands it does not explain why only a minority of those exposed to the 'unfavourable social conditions' he enumerates do in fact succumb to delinquency. Healy and Bronner would say that the answer lies in the relationships within each individual family.

D. H. Stott sees the emotional difficulties and behaviour troubles of young people arising from their being 'starved' of one or both of two primary human needs.[12], [13] One of these is the need to attach oneself to a small permanent group whose members feel warmly towards each other and in which one is accepted without question. For the child this group is the family. The other need centres around the feeling of counting for something, of having some status or capacity for achievement.

Where a child finds his primary needs are not being met, anxiety may arise. Stott illustrates as anxiety the feeling people get when a member of the family is unaccountably late home; a kind of fretful restlessness. He says this restlessness becomes chronic in children who have been subjected to long periods of 'family-insecurity'. He has isolated a number of family situations which can give rise to anxiety in the child and thus perhaps lead to delinquency. Each one of these situations involves unsatisfactory emotional relationships with one or both parents, ranging from uncertainty about parental love to outright rejection by the parents. Even if Stott does not use his research material with precise scientific accuracy, his observations have real meaning for practical social workers. When he turns to a discussion of means for resolving unsatisfactory family situations, however, we are less enthusiastic. He postulates a family therapist who will be able to modify emotional situations by logical argument while not becoming emotionally involved in any way. We feel that such a person and such a method have little basis in reality.

Stott is supported in some of his beliefs by Dr John Bowlby, who is associated principally with work on the so-called affectionless character.[14], [15] He sees the affectionless character as the persistent delinquent, and believes that this type of character develops from maternal deprivation of a special kind – prolonged separation from mother or foster-mother during infancy. Bowlby's use of his material has not entirely satisfied the scientific purists, but the social worker finds in his conclusions much that ties in with his own experience.

To summarize the position we have reached so far, lack of love and absence of acceptance within the family, or lack of certainty about love and about acceptance seem to be a common factor in the theories of Healy and Bronner, Stott and Bowlby. Insecurity and anxiety are engendered thereby, which may lead to delinquency. Bovet has common ground with this, although he sees the causes of anxiety as arising sometimes from situations outside the family. He bridges the gap between this line of thought and the ecological school which emphasizes the social factors impinging upon the delinquent. Mays' attempt to distinguish between the casually delinquent and the persistently anti-social person is important. We must also recognize with Morris that since the family is the main means of transmitting cultural values and is the main agency of social control, the difference between the standards and training of 'working-class' and 'middle-class' families is important.

Is it possible to reconcile these ideas with the theory that emotional immaturity is associated with delinquency? Dr W. F. Roper in his studies of prisoners at Wakefield prison[16] confirmed the social worker's long-held but unsubstantiated belief that many persistent offenders are emotionally immature. Maturity in the emotional sense involves such conceptions as the capacity for giving love as well as demanding it; for making helpful, friendly and enduring relationships with others; and for awaiting the fulfilment of personal satisfactions with due regard for the realities of the situation and the needs of others. Whatever the difficulties of precise definition, the conception is undoubtedly a valid one. We believe that an individual progresses towards emotional maturity only when he has a family setting in which it is possible for him to do so. It follows that deficiencies in family relationships are the chief factors which retard the emotional development of the persistent offender.

Sheldon and Eleanor Glueck, the American criminologists, lend their considerable authority to the idea that delinquency and emotional immaturity are related.[17] In a later work[18] they base upon relationships within the family a table for predicting delinquency in juveniles.

It appears, then, that whether the delinquent is seen as

unloved, as a sufferer from anxiety, or as emotionally immature, the weight of modern thought is behind the idea that the roots of delinquency lie in the family and its relationships. It is very clear that some consideration must be given to the inherited factors in each individual and also to his social environment. But the social worker cannot alter the one, and, apart from recommending the removal of the delinquent, has only a minor direct influence over the other. With the necessarily limited aim of dealing with the delinquent in his ordinary environment, it is principally to the family and to the relationships within it that he will turn his attention for a working understanding of what has gone wrong.

This is what the experienced social worker already does. But what form should his relationship with the delinquent and his family take? The American 'casework' school has approached this in broad terms,[19], [20] but the criminologists, with the exception of Stott, are largely silent on the subject. For the social worker the question is a fundamental one, and it will be our concern throughout this book.

III

Diagnosing Delinquency

Our conclusion in the last chapter was that the social worker must turn his attention principally to the family and the relationships within it for a working understanding of the delinquent. We said that the question of the form that his relationship with the delinquent and his family should take was a fundamental one. To enable us to pursue this, it is necessary to look a little more closely at the significance of the delinquent act itself.

It is often said that in the commission of a delinquent act there are both predisposing and precipitating factors.[21] It is usually extremely difficult to distinguish one from the other, but the conception is useful. The predisposing factors may be regarded as those which have induced in the delinquent a susceptibility to crime. Such factors in our view stem largely from the family and its relationships. The precipitating factors are those which seem to give rise to the immediate delinquent act. They are connected mainly with environment, companionship, and opportunity.

A simple statement of this concept of predisposing and precipitating factors would be that a predisposition to delinquency makes the individual more easily affected by the precipitating factors. His 'defences' against delinquency – moral, emotional, and intellectual – are not so strong as those of most people, and thus in certain circumstances they are more easily overcome. It is generally agreed that the 'defences' of even perfectly normal children and adolescents are lower than those of adults.

It is true of course that a person who seems to have normal defences against delinquency may still commit a delinquent act. Such a person has been described as 'casually' delinquent, and usually he does not repeat his delinquency. He and others like him swell the criminal statistics, but they do not become persistent offenders. Dr Grünhut has found that, in juveniles, the frequency with which such offenders appear before the court varies from area to area[22]. This might reflect local conditions but could also be an indication of variations in police policy in the matter of cautioning.

Those who are casually delinquent may be deterred by punishment or even by threat of punishment, but they can also be helped by social workers. Often quite a large proportion of the cases dealt with by a probation officer may be in this category. His representation of authority, his reminder, of society's warning, and his friendly interest are sometimes all that is required. If correct selection could be guaranteed, those children who are dealt with by police liaison officers would be of this kind. The difficulty is to decide initially upon those who are more than casually delinquent. For this reason, the social worker must bring an open and inquiring mind to his contact with every delinquent. Although the worker can be of some help to the casually delinquent, it is nevertheless with the individual predisposed to delinquency that his most intensive work will lie.

When he is looking at relationships between members of a family in his effort to understand predisposing factors, he is looking at feelings. It is important to emphasize at this point – though it is certainly a truism to many people – that human feelings exist at varying levels. We can be conscious of some of our own feelings, but not of others.

Conscious feelings are obviously often expressed in action. Anger may lead to a punch, affection to a kiss. Unconscious feelings may also motivate behaviour but the person concerned will not immediately be aware of it. Freud, the original explorer of the unconscious mind, tells us 'You cannot . . . get round the fact that acts of a mental nature, often very complicated, go on in you without you being conscious of them'.[23]

One does not need to follow Freud in all his doctrines to accept this. The idea of unconscious motivation is common to all the main schools of psychological thought. Once it has been pointed out, it is recognized as part of normal experience. The feelings in children which lead to persistent nail-biting, or rocking or head-banging, for instance, are clearly not conscious to the children concerned. They cannot explain the reason for their behaviour, and usually cannot stop it by a conscious effort of will. Again, people who are very particular about cleanliness can normally give a rational justification for this. Where, however, they go so far as to wash their hands every hour, such justification sounds thin and we look for an unconscious motivation.

In the category of bizarre behaviour, unconscious motivation is acceptable enough to most people. They can recognize it in men who have a persistent urge to slash women's mackintoshes or to snip off girls' hair: to smash plate-glass windows or to spy on courting couples. With apparently normal offences, such as theft, people are less ready to accept it because a seemingly conscious, rational motive, such as greed, lies immediately to hand.

We discussed in the previous chapter the idea of 'anxiety' – in a special sense – as being a factor in delinquent behaviour. This anxiety seemed to arise from emotional situations within the family. It would not be consciously conceived and understood by the person experiencing it. He would be 'driven' by it unconsciously. It would 'drive' him into actions, sometimes delinquent actions, which he would not always be able to explain. He might think he knew why he had behaved as he had – he might even give quite logical and credible reasons for such behaviour. Fundamentally, however, they might not be the true explanation. He might, for example, say he had acted in this way because he wanted some excitement, without realizing that there was an unconscious motive which made him need to have this excitement.

Some delinquents when asked why they committed their offence say 'I don't know'. This is particularly so with children and very often it is true. Even if they know the simple precipitating factors they certainly have no knowledge of the underlying feelings which motivated them. Adult offenders sometimes say 'I can't think why I did it', or 'I can't understand what came over me'. This too is, more often than is generally realized, an accurate statement of the situation.

Within the family there will be some feelings which are farther from consciousness than others. It will help to look at an example in which the parents of a sixteen-year-old girl come to see a social worker because they are worried about the girl's behaviour. They say at once that they love their daughter, and this appears to be true, for they shower gifts upon her. But the feelings which prompt them to give her these presents may not stem from love. The parents may unconsciously feel guilty because they do not and possibly cannot give their daughter the real love which they sense is the right and proper emotion. If they are to be assisted, and the daughter also, these feelings of guilt have to be looked at by them with the assistance of another person who can help them to understand something of the meaning of such feelings.

As the social worker's experience is enlarged, he becomes increasingly aware of unconscious feelings in others. He distinguishes 'real' and 'presented' problems, meaning that the problem as the client comprehends it and presents it may not be the real one. Unconscious feelings of which he is obviously unaware are motivating him. It is sometimes the task of the social worker to help his client to reach some understanding about feelings of which he is at first not fully conscious. We shall, in the course of discussing treatment and case-histories, speak of 'deep' or 'underlying' or 'real' problems or feelings, by which we shall mean those of the kind we have outlined above.

To understand more easily what has been said so far in this chapter, it will be helpful to consider an actual offence and to discuss some of the feelings at various levels of consciousness which may have contributed to it. Quite simply, a boy of thirteen years has stolen five shillings from his teacher's desk. What might have led him to do this?

First of all there is the obvious motive of greed for anything he could get, or a more directed greed for something he wanted to buy with the money. In a less inquiring age, this sort of motive was thought to be the main driving force behind theft. But supposing the boy had only a week ago handed to his headmaster a ten-shilling note which he had found in the playground, and could quite easily have kept. This would take our attention from the object stolen to a more careful consideration of the person from whom it was stolen. Could it be that in stealing from a teacher – probably more hazardous than keeping money found in the playground – the boy was showing a personal dislike for the teacher concerned? The possibility is there, but it is also possible that he was moved by unconscious feelings – unconscious hostility perhaps against authority in general. It has been found that such hostility is often grounded in early angry feelings against the father, which have never been overcome and are transferred to the teacher as representing the father symbolically.

If neither of these theories can be reconciled with other facts known about the boy, then attention might next be directed towards what he actually did with the money he had stolen. Supposing he spent it on sweets which he handed round freely to other boys in his class. One might surmise then that he was buying friendship; trying to gain popularity or esteem which he felt he was unable to obtain in the ordinary way. This might be a conscious enough motive, but underlying it would be the unconscious feeling of unworthiness which led him to believe he was not likable for his own sake. This sort of general feeling of unworthiness often has its roots in an insecure emotional feeling about family affection.

Supposing, however, it is found out that other boys in the class have also been stealing recently. It might then be that the delinquent in question stole because he wanted to be accepted as one of a gang. He might even have done it as a bold piece of wrong-doing which would establish his right to lead the gang. These would be his overt motives. Underlying them would be unconscious needs – needs perhaps for security, acceptance, dominance and excitement, which were met by gang-membership or gang-leadership. Again these are likely to have their origin in his feelings about lack of acceptance within his family.

Let us imagine that, in reviewing the history of the thief, it is learnt that he has been a persistent pilferer for several years. In such circumstances the social worker ought to look immediately at the boy's family life. Such chronic light-fingeredness often springs from the delinquent's long-standing anxiety regarding his position in the family. Family deficiencies with regard to interest and affection are sometimes obvious to someone outside the family. If these are not so obvious, then the social worker will look at other details. Does the boy eat enormously, perhaps cramming himself with jam and chocolate? Did he spend the whole five shillings on sweets which he ate himself? These are classic symptoms of affection-craving; they are a way of expressing unconscious feelings which cannot be shown directly.

How did the boy react when his theft was discovered? This is another important factor in the consideration of superficial and underlying motives. Supposing he showed no apprehension about punishment or the future, or even about being removed from his home. In this event, it might be felt that his need for affection had been so long and so completely unmet that he had given up the unconscious assertion of his right to it;

34

he had indeed suppressed his right to enjoy any feeling at all. He might thus be in the category of Bowlby's 'affectionless character'.

Supposing, on the other hand, he had stolen from a teacher for whom he had previously shown a strong liking and who liked him. When people steal from those who they feel are fond of them, then the motive again is an unconscious one. It is thought to be a form of 'testing-out' by those who are unconsciously uncertain whether they can be loved at all: to prove that they are liked or loved even if they are as bad as they fear.

Lastly, consideration must be given to the way in which the theft was actually carried out. If it was done with a skill or cunning appropriate to the boy's age and intelligence, then investigation on these lines need go no further. But the theft might be done so obviously that the thief would inevitably be detected. Such thefts occur more frequently than one might think. They seem to indicate an unconscious wish on the part of the delinquent to be discovered and punished. The origin of this wish, according to Freud, lies in guilt feelings deriving from unconscious hostile feelings against the father.

There is much more that could be said about this one case. We have expressly avoided any reference to methods of dealing with the offender. Our intention is to establish that delinquents are not a simple homogeneous group and that their motives are varied and involve both conscious and unconscious feelings. In a later chapter we shall be discussing other types of offences and some of the feelings that seem to lie behind them.

In stating that earlier and current feelings within a

delinquent's family may predispose him towards delinquency, it might be thought that we are going further and saying that they are a *cause* of his delinquency. This is a step we are not prepared to take. Sometimes it seems that all the predisposing factors are there but the person is not delinquent. It is much more useful to say that certain family emotional situations are often *associated with* delinquent behaviour in some members of that family. This gives the social worker a theoretical framework for his operations. We can now go on to see what those operations involve.

IV

Approach to Treatment

An old, discarded theory of crime was that some people were born criminals. Lombroso, writing in the mid-nineteenth century, believed he had identified certain physical stigmata by which the hereditary criminal could be identified. Discredited as these theories are, Lombroso made a vital contribution to criminology in as much as he directed attention towards the individual criminal. Since Lombroso's day there have been many detailed studies of the life-history of individual criminals. Expressed in the words of Alfred Adler, one major school of thought holds that 'if you trace back the life of a criminal, you will almost always find that the trouble began in his early family life.'[24] We have put this into more modern, and we think more acceptable, dress in the last paragraph of the preceding chapter.

The idea may seem a pessimistic one. How can even the youthful criminal go back and relive his life differently? If he cannot do that, his attitude to society and to his fellows cannot, apparently, be altered. Crime would therefore seem incurable. On the other hand it may be suggested that, if the criminal associates punishment with crime and at the same time learns to associate good behaviour with desirable things like community approval, he will not offend again. Many of society's remedies against crime listed in Chapter I have their basis in this idea. Certainly these social controls

-- fear of punishment and social pressure to conform -- seem to work well enough with the normal, well-adjusted citizen.

The social worker knows from experience, however, that they are increasingly unavailing in proportion to the maladjustment of the person concerned, but this does not lead him to think that crime is incurable. What is needed, and what he believes in some cases he can provide, is a method of helping those who are less amenable to social controls. Such a method can help to achieve an adjustment of attitudes whereby such people can become more satisfactory both to society and to themselves. This is the 'treatment by social worker' of which we have already spoken.

At this stage it seems important to say that this attempt at an adjustment of attitudes may include the use of normal social controls. Contact with the social worker is in itself a form of control. He can explain and sometimes represent the demands of society. He tries to do this in a way acceptable to the individual delinquent with whom he is dealing. With the less disturbed people this may be all that the social worker needs to do. In other cases something more is required, and we may now look in closer detail at the sort of action the social worker may take in differing situations.

In one way the social worker may be seen as attempting to work with the delinquent in meeting a need which the delinquent is unable to meet on his own. The need may be a material one, such as for bedding, clothing, lodgings, or employment. This is the purely welfare aspect of the social worker's function. Alternatively, the need may be for a change of environment. This may also be met as a welfare need, but, if it involves changing the family background, it may mean more than this. The social worker may in fact attempt to help the family to alter its attitudes to the individual concerned. Here we are in the realm of emotional readjustment. Where the need of the delinquent seems to be a modification of his attitude to his environment – to family, employer, friends, or to society in general – then emotional readjustments become the paramount consideration.

Material provision, change in the delinquent's environment, and readjustment of the delinquent's attitude to his environment: social workers are accustomed to working in these three ways at the same time; advancing, that is, on all three fronts simultaneously.

However it is analysed, the work requires a certain manner of approach. The social worker must work *with* the delinquent. This is very different from what is commonly supposed to happen. The popular conception is that the social worker gives – whether it be goods, money, advice or correction – and the individual in need merely takes. Perhaps indeed this does sometimes still happen, but in its fullest sense social work with individuals demands a joint endeavour. In work with delinquents it may not always begin in this way. The delinquent will often not see the situation in that light. Indeed he may never quite come to see himself with a need in exactly the sense in which the social worker understands it. Nevertheless the aim is co-operation.

In welfare provision and environmental changes of a physical nature, just as much as in readjustments of attitude, the social worker again should try to work with the delinquent and not just for him. Experience has shown that the delinquent himself should usually be aware of the need for changes if they are to be fully effective in altering his behaviour. Particularly is this so with adults. In the ideal situation, the delinquent himself is so helped that he himself is capable of bringing about the change. The degree to which this is possible varies with the age and maturity of the individual concerned, but planning *with* him should always be the aim.

To adopt such an approach to the delinquent is not so simple as it sounds. People who are in positions of authority – for example probation officers and teachers – are particularly open to the mistake of planning for rather than with the person they wish to help. They think they can see what is good for him: he must get more regular employment; he must try to get a council house; he must give his wife more money; he must help his wife more with the children; he must smarten up his appearance; he must sell the car which he cannot afford; he must save money. When one or more of these needs is so clearly seen, it is a short and insidious step for the social worker to impose them upon the person he wants to help. He may know influential people in the neighbourhood who can get them met quickly. Letters to these people are sent, telephone calls are made to other social workers. The delinquent is greeted with admonition and exhortation when he sees the social worker. He is sometimes met with commands, but a sort of friendly persuasion is probably more common: 'What you want to do is . . .' or 'If I were you I should . . .'

Quite often however, this approach gets nowhere, because, although the plan envisaged would be effective for the social worker himself if his were the need, it does not apply to the delinquent, as he is at present. The true task of the social worker is to see, to feel with, to work with the delinquent as he actually is and not as the social worker might think he should be. For example, to take an extreme case, how many plans for tramps to get work, to settle down, and to be clean and smart, have been blown sky high within twenty-four hours of their making? Very many, and we have learnt from bitter experience that plans and changes in the making of which the delinquent himself is not directly consulted are not likely to succeed. The more comprehensive the plan, the greater the likelihood of failure. Initially at any rate, the social worker's aims in attempting treatment should be tentative and limited. Above all they should be within the capacity of the person they concern.

It may be thought that in discouraging planning and provision *for* the delinquent we are advocating a form of professional unconcern, even inhumanity. It is easy to think this. The social worker, when confronted with people in need of adequate clothing, housing or work, for example, may well see his immediate task to lie in supplying these needs. 'You cannot moralize with a hungry man' is a common statement justifying this, and it is a valid one. But as we have already tried to show, where there is need the social worker must do more than just meet it in the way he himself thinks proper. He must provide in a manner and a form that the delinquent can accept. In addition, he must consider why it is that the individual concerned has been unable to meet his own needs. Further still, his ultimate aim must lie in helping the delinquent to a position in which he *is* able to do so for himself.

Social workers seem naturally eager to deal with practical situations. Often they are very good at it. They find work for people, find lodgings, get them

41

loans or grants, get them to forgive each other, even if only temporarily. Much of this, indeed, is inevitably temporary; it will only be of lasting value if it leads to an attempt at understanding the individual involved in the situation.

How does one understand another person? Basically, it is an attempt to see what induces the individual to behave as he does. This demands a study of his environment and his family; of how and where he grew up. It also demands a knowledge of his feelings about the important people and events in his life, not only at the present time, but also in the past. In addition, it requires an understanding of his feelings about his present situation, his offence, and about the social worker himself.

The facts acquired in this sort of exercise are important, but so too is the exercise itself. If it is carried out sensitively and without haste, it demonstrates real concern for the delinquent. An attempt to understand someone can of itself be helpful in indicating that the social worker values the person concerned as an individual, even if it is not very successful and leads to no overt action. It may, as we shall see later, be the beginning of change for the better in some people.

We have gone a little way in this chapter towards understanding the way in which the social worker approaches his attempt at treatment. In the next chapter we shall look somewhat more deeply at the underlying theory.

V

The Essential Relationship

How does one attempt to help someone else to achieve a permanent alteration in behaviour? If attitudes are reflected in behaviour, such an attempt must involve a readjustment of those attitudes towards family, employment, authority, or the community generally. This must seem very difficult, and it appears to run contrary to our society's conventional beliefs. It is part of our folk-wisdom that a leopard doesn't change its spots. The question is commonly asked: 'Is he honest?', not 'Has he been honest?' or 'Will he be honest?' It is rather as if we are being asked 'Is he tall?' or 'Is he left-handed?' The assumption is that people do not change. But social workers know that they *do*. How does this come about?

Interest in the individual, and concern for him, is usually the beginning. In the last chapter we suggested that the attempt to understand the delinquent was one means of conveying the social worker's interest and concern. Material help if necessary and general planning with the delinquent are further evidence of this interest and concern. The result may be the development of a relationship between helper and helped within which the helped person can learn to feel valued and worthwhile. As this relationship develops, the social worker in some cases may be able to go even further. The delinquent may be able to understand something of himself, something of his behaviour, and of the attitudes which lie behind it. The relationship may help the delinquent to mature emotionally, so that he may react to people and to situations in a more realistic and adult manner.

Important as this is, it is still only a part of the story. The delinquent is not usually dealt with in isolation. The social worker will in many cases also have an impact upon the delinquent's family and, perhaps to a lesser extent, upon other areas of his social environment, such as school or employment.

A simple definition of a relationship is that it exists when two people have continuing feelings about each other. The feelings flow in both directions, and are not necessarily all loving, grateful and kindly. There will be hostile feelings too, although they may not always be overtly expressed. The feelings of the social worker may sometimes be critical and angry. If he is in the authoritative position of teacher, club-leader or probation officer, he will sometimes need to chide and correct. Criticism, correction, and reproof, given within a secure relationship, may strengthen the bond between social worker and delinquent. Anger itself does not kill a good relationship any more than it destroys the tie between parent and child. But the anger of the social worker must be controlled. It must be used in the right place and with the right person. Here lies the skill. It must not represent the instinctive gratification of the social worker's own emotions. This should be left to his private life.

The relationship between the social worker and the delinquent rests on a delicate point of balance. It is a balance between approval and criticism; between kindness and firmness; between warning and promise; between love and temporary withholding of love. To create and maintain such a relationship might seem a task only for a highly-trained expert. This in fact is not so. Training and experience are necessary, but the interest and concern which lie at the centre of all such relationships stem from the hearts of quite ordinary people. That is probably why social workers sometimes succeed in cases in which highly skilled psychiatrists fail. It is why, despite the increasingly professional outlook of the social worker – valuable and necessary as this may be – and despite the conscious development of skill, his individual personality is still of paramount importance.

It may be helpful if we look a little more deeply at the theoretical implications of the relationship.

We accept that, after taking into account what he brings with him into the world at birth, the delinquent's attitudes to people and situations are largely the result of his early emotional relationships, principally within his family. We shall discuss this further in a later chapter. A simple exposition of this has also been made by the authors in a previous work.[1]

The effecting of any significant readjustment in these attitudes must in some way involve new relationships to replace or modify the earlier ones. We have learnt from our own experience and from the experience of others that a relationship with a social worker can sometimes bring about a change of attitudes in an individual. Thus it must be that in some way the social worker, by means of this relationship, gives the other a chance to achieve some form of emotional 'reshuffle'. He enables the delinquent to relive – symbolically perhaps – in a more satisfying way those early relationships which were unsuccessful, inasmuch as through them delinquent attitudes were developed.

In discussing psychotherapy, Alfred Adler said: 'The

task of the physician or psychologist is to give the patient the contact with a fellow-man and then enable him to transfer this awakened social interest to others. This method of winning the patient's good will and then transferring it to his environment is strictly analogous to the function of the mother, whose social task is to interpret society to the individual'.[24] This statement seems immediately relevant to the relationship aspect of the social worker's task. We noticed in our excursion into the aetiology of delinquency in Chapter II that the delinquent person may frequently be identified with the immature person. The immature person, because of his unsatisfactory early emotional experiences, is unable to relate himself realistically and in an adult way to others. If such a person can be helped to make one successful relationship – with the social worker – then he may be encouraged to go on and make others. Each further successful relationship is a step towards emotional maturity.

We have suggested that the relationship between the social worker and the delinquent enables the latter to re-experience more successfully the emotions involved in his early family relationships. Perhaps we could express it more acceptably if we said that a curative relationship for the delinquent is one in which he can deal afresh with his hating and loving feelings; one in which he can have an object for these feelings in a person who is neither destroyed nor overwhelmed by them and who shows concern, interest and consistency in spite of them.

However little the social worker in a particular case may feel he has 'done', if a relationship like this has developed, the basis of useful treatment is there.

It would be wrong to imply that *all* delinquents need the same depth of relationship with the social worker. Nor would we suggest that the social worker can always be expected to achieve the sort of relationship he aims at. Having said this, it may be useful now – and perhaps reassuring to those who feel we are advocating something very difficult – to consider in detail the various levels at which the social worker may work with different individuals, bearing in mind that some sort of a relationship is a basic necessity.

The social worker functions both in representing and in explaining the social demands of society. He will do this as much by his general attitude as by what he actually says.

We all need encouragement and support at times, but some people need it more than others. How common is the child's cry: 'Watch me, Mummy', or 'Daddy, come and see what I've done'. The immaturity of many delinquents is apparent, however grown-up they are physically. Child or adult, the delinquent is often in need of encouragement, and the social worker is well-placed to provide it. This playing of what has been called the 'supportive role' may in some cases be all that is required. Each interview consists simply of the social worker listening as approvingly as possible to the delinquent's account of his recent achievements. This approval can enable the delinquent to go on to do increasingly more constructive things.

Sometimes the delinquent feels himself to be quite a bad person whom nobody could like. Concern for him, coupled with this reasonable approval from the social worker, can help him to feel more worthwhile. Many social workers treat the delinquent as a better person than he really is. This may appear starry-eyed, but in many cases it proves effective. For some social workers it is undoubtedly a conscious technique. Others, however, do it naturally and unconsciously, and this has its dangers, since not all cases will respond and it is necessary to select with care the people who may be helped by this method.

Another function of the social worker may be described as clarification. This involves helping the delinquent to understand a little more about himself; about his position in his family, at work or at school, and among his friends. It can enable him to see perhaps a little more objectively how he responds to other people and how they see and react to him, to see something of his life-pattern. Clarification in the technical sense in which we are using it, is on the normal level of rational discussion. The hope is that having seen in a clearer light some of the less satisfactory aspects of his behaviour, the delinquent will be able to make conscious adjustments. For the less disturbed individual, and particularly for the adolescent whose delinquency represents an exaggerated revolt against his parents, this clarifying process may be effective.

The representation of the demands of society, welfare provision, support and approval, clarification: all these may be carried on with one individual in a combined process, and we isolate them only for the purpose of exposition. At the same time, the 'treatment' may go on at a deeper level. We have already tried to show something of the deeper processes within the relationship and these are of fundamental importance in cases which are worked at any depth.

We have not yet suggested, however, that the social

worker should make any attempt to put into words in an interview the unconscious significance of what takes place. It may of course be that he himself will have little insight into this, but this will not necessarily make his work any the less valuable. However, with experience and training, he may feel able in certain cases to give additional help at this deeper level. We do not mean that he should attempt to interpret in the psycho-analytic manner the delinquent's unconscious motivations. This is highly skilled work which it is wiser to leave to the psychoanalyst.

What the social worker may be able to do, once a relationship has been established, is to enable the delinquent to talk about his bad feelings without thinking himself condemned. This tacit acceptance of underlying feelings can be very helpful. In addition, if the setting and atmosphere are right, the delinquent may be enabled to use the social worker as a means by which he, the delinquent, can tell himself things about himself which have hitherto been hidden just below the level of consciousness. He tells himself as he tells the social worker, and the social worker's skill in this situation lies in putting back to him in different words, or re-emphasizing in the same words, just what it is he has said. The social worker may sometimes be able to go even further and link up different remarks the delinquent has made and put them back to him so that their underlying significance is apparent.

Jung described the process thus: 'Most people need a *vis-à-vis*, otherwise the basis of experience is not sufficiently real. Otherwise the individual cannot "hear" himself and has no opportunity of contrasting himself in order to ascertain what he himself really is.'[25] The social worker, in work at this level, is the delinquent's *vis-à-vis*. He is the instrument by which the delinquent is helped to a fuller understanding of his own feelings; he is the means by which the delinquent is enabled in some degree to come to terms with his real self.

VI

The Social Worker and the Family

In the previous chapter we concentrated our attention upon the social worker's relationship with the delinquent. Although this is an important part of the treatment, it is not the whole of it in most cases. A delinquent is usually a member of a family group. The emotional attitudes within that group we have already seen as fundamental, not only in developing but also in maintaining the attitudes of the delinquent to individuals and to society in general. Thus it is that the impact of the social worker upon the delinquent's family is usually important and in some cases vital.

We shall be looking in detail in the next chapter at the kind of emotions and situations in the family which may lead to the delinquency of one or more of its members. Here we shall discuss the kind of approach by the social worker which is likely to be effective in dealing with the delinquent's family. At this point a distinction must be drawn between work with adults and with children. With adults, the social worker is more likely to concentrate upon the delinquent himself. Often he does not need to concern himself with the parents because they are no longer directly influencing the individual person: they may even be dead. What the worker may do, if the case requires it, is to help the delinquent to deal with the loving and hating feelings basically conditioned by the early relationship with his parents or substitute-parents, or with his brothers and sisters.

Where the adult delinquent is married the situation is different again. It may be helpful to work with the spouse in some cases, but careful thought is required before attempting this. Of paramount importance is the way in which the delinquent's wife or husband – as the case may be – views the social worker. He may represent to some people an affront to their feelings of respectability or a constant reminder of the shame occasioned by the offence. Where this is so, the social worker's contact with the family may seem to the offender a continual re-opening of an old wound, or a repeated belittlement of himself in the eyes of his spouse, and of his children if they are old enough to understand. These feelings can usually be discussed with the delinquent and, where this is possible, it may be that social worker and delinquent can move on by this means to greater understanding. It may sometimes be wiser to give up seeing the family altogether if such visits seem to arouse anxiety or resentment.

With some delinquents, contact with the wife or husband may be seen immediately as a demonstration of interest and concern. Where this is so, assistance in the form of support and encouragement can obviously be given. Again, to a lonely old couple, the social worker's relationship with both partners may represent friendship and sympathetic warmth, and coming from a younger person this will be greatly valued. The variation in circumstances and response is extremely wide. In his approach to the delinquent's family, therefore, as in other aspects of his work, the social worker needs both sensitivity and flexibility.

With the younger delinquent, the family may still

constitute the main background to life. The relationships within it have shaped his attitudes and may continue to do so. If then, in however small a degree, the social worker can influence relationships within the family, and particularly between the delinquent and other members of it, the effect may sometimes be considerable.

Initially, he will not always necessarily be seen by the family as a helpful person. From the parents he must be prepared sometimes for anger or hostility, sometimes for anxiety and fear. He may also encounter guilt and dependence. Whatever the early feelings, his aim will as always be to get a good relationship with them. A good relationship, as we have seen, does not mean one in which gratitude and good-will are the only feelings expressed; all emotions must be taken into account. A relationship in which the parents have strong, though perhaps changing, feelings and in which the social worker's feelings are also involved, is probably the most effective.

However, work with all families may not be at a deep level of feeling. The demonstrated interest of the social worker may be all that is required. His personal concern for the family and its delinquent member may be sufficient for them to rediscover more positive feelings for each other. It may be that the parents' interest is re-awakened when they see a stranger interested. The sympathy and understanding of the social worker can often be very effective with the care-worn, over-burdened mother who has 'given up' and let things slide. If the social worker shows that he thinks her worthwhile, she may begin to think so herself and ultimately recover some of her self-respect and pride. From this the whole family can benefit.

The social worker must make up his mind fairly soon to what extent he is working generally with the whole family and to what extent with the delinquent only. There is a balance here which is different in every case. With some the social worker may be working almost entirely by means of the family. This will apply more often with very young delinquents. In other cases, at the opposite extreme, he may feel that the family has little influence on the delinquent and that he must deal with him largely in isolation or in co-operation with agencies outside the family, such as school or employment. The majority of cases involving youthful delinquents will probably fall between these extremes.

Normally the key members of the delinquent's family, so far as he is concerned, are his parents. It is from them that he should get the love, security, encouragement and control which will enable him to develop towards a stable emotional maturity. It is mainly from them too that he gains his conception of masculinity and femininity, and the sort of behaviour which is appropriate to each. He absorbs from them, partly unconsciously, his ideas of how fathers and mothers and husbands and wives should behave.

When the social worker comes upon the scene, it may be that the younger delinquent will see in him something of a parent. Initially, perhaps the delinquent will carry over into the new relationship something of his feelings for his father – or mother if the social worker is female. On the social worker's side, it is equally likely that he will take on something of the role of parent. Many social workers see themselves as 'good parents' to their delinquents. Inexperienced workers may accept this role unconsciously. The next insidious step is to attempt to prove themselves better 'parents' than the parents themselves. This can even lead to an attempt to take away the loyalty of the delinquent from his own parents. Such an attempt will rarely succeed and in any case is unhelpful, for the delinquent's real need is usually a feeling of security and happiness within his own family.

This situation is more subtly difficult with the adolescent. More often than not he is at some stage in some degree of revolt against the standards and attitudes of his parents. He may not, however, be against his parents personally, which can add to his confusion. He is ready for constructive relationships with adults outside his family. Quite often in normal development he is readier to accept influence from someone else he respects than from his own parents. With some delinquents the normal adolescent revolt is exaggerated. Then he may accept only the standards of his gang or crowd. Sometimes, however, he is ready for a sustained and helpful relationship with a social worker. Because the social worker is then in such a strong position to give support and guidance, he should take extra care not to cut the parents out altogether. He may feel they have failed their child, but his proper task notwithstanding is to help both delinquent and parents through this difficult stage; to help the delinquent develop his individual personality and at the same time to try to make the family bond more effective.

The social worker can help even the younger delinquent to come to terms with his loving and hating feelings through their relationship. The question is whether he can assist the process in suitable cases through his influence with the delinquent's family. Again he will do it through the relationship he is able to develop –

this time with the parents. Let us say for example that it is the father who the social worker feels is not giving his delinquent son the interest and affection he needs. How does he deal with the situation? Straightforwardly telling the father is very unlikely to achieve anything but anger. People are very seldom able to learn about themselves in this way. A more hopeful approach, as we saw when we were discussing the social worker's impact upon the delinquent himself, is to let the father use the social worker as a means of revealing something of himself to himself. An example may illustrate the method.

John was fifteen. He was big for his age and a little above average intelligence. He was in the C stream at his grammar school. One night, using a key which he had manufactured, he entered his school physics laboratory and stole some test-tubes, a thermometer and a stop-watch. The headmaster called in the police on learning of the burglary, and since John had boasted of his exploit to his form-mates it was not long before he was questioned and charged by the detective-sergeant. His subsequent court appearance was a great shock to his respectable parents. His father, a commerical traveller, was 'too busy' to attend the court. His mother, however, came looking very well-dressed and told the magistrates that she couldn't understand John's behaviour, because he had always been such a good boy. John looked suitably contrite throughout the proceedings, said he was sorry for what he had done, and was placed on probation for two years.

His work at school was not very good, so his parents wished to remove him, believing in any case that the disgrace made this necessary. The headmaster did nothing to influence them against this course, as he thought that John was not up to the standard of most of the other boys. The probation officer soon realised that this was wise. It was clear that John's intelligence had only just been sufficient to gain him a grammar school place, with the constant 'pushing' of his parents. He certainly did not possess the mental equipment to attain the high standards expected of him by his parents. His mother had required and endeavoured to enforce high standards of behaviour in other respects too – in cleanliness, smartness of dress, punctuality, and in constructive leisure pursuits. Whatever John did was never quite good enough for her. Getting no appreciation at home and being unable to earn it at school by scholastic ability or skill at games, John had tried to acquire the regard of his school-mates by general buffoonery.

It seemed easy and natural for the probation officer to give the boy a measure of encouragement, which seemed to be needed. He listened to John's accounts of his moderate achievements in his new job as an office junior and gave approval and occasional praise. His main, and perhaps less obvious work lay with the parents, and particularly with John's mother. The shock of the court appearance had precipitated in her a readiness to think again about her attitude to her son. She began to see now how over-demanding she had been. Within a carefully developed relationship, the probation officer did his best to encourage this new attitude. He called upon her regularly, listened to her self-criticism and occasionally put back to her the meaning behind what she said, using more or less the words she had used herself. Soon she was telling him – and herself – that she and her husband had never praised John, had never given

57

him credit for anything, had never made him feel worth-while at all. She imparted some of these new feelings to her husband, and the new spirit of acceptance and support was communicated to John in many ways. It was after a fight with another lad in the park, when his father for the first time accepted his side of the story, that John proudly told the probation officer: 'My dad was on my side.' After that his behaviour showed a steady improvement in every way and he did not offend again.

John's association with the probation officer was help-ful, but it is unlikely that the case would have gone so well if it had not been for the probation officer's relation-ship with the mother, which enabled her to 'hear' herself and thereby understand feelings which had been concealed even from herself.

VII

The Delinquent and his Family

From the foregoing chapters it is evident that the early life and relationships of the delinquent must be studied to try to find how attitudes arose which produced delinquent acts. The patterns of family feeling contribute to the production of a personality which may be more or less disposed to delinquent actions. These patterns are not within the control of the individual himself and much depends upon those who are around him in early infancy, and through childhood.

Discussion of the development of the personality in the present book can only be superficial, but there is a simple study of this to which the reader is referred.[26] Here we confine ourselves to looking at some examples of the way in which the social worker may be able to spot defective relationships in the family, and to consideration of some of the family situations frequently encountered and some of the problems most frequently raised.

In any family group, the growing child will find that frustrating situations arise in which he will feel thwarted. Indeed, it may reasonably be asserted that in some ways this process of growing-up is a denial of the instinctive feelings and actions of the child. In another sense it is a necessary adjustment of his feelings and actions to the demands of society as represented by the family. Everyone must learn to deal with frustration and control in some form or other, and extreme parental

59

permissiveness will usually produce children who are not easily tolerated by their fellows.

Most people unconsciously achieve some emotional adjustment to the conflicts which arise in the give-and-take of family life. Such adjustment will vary with each individual, and in dealing with the delinquent we shall usually be concerned with a person in whom these adjustments have been unsatisfactory to a greater or lesser degree. We have already made it clear that social workers are not psycho-analysts and will not need to try to reveal the deepest unconscious feelings of their clients. They should, however, be aware of the existence of such feelings and of their possible origins in the family relationships.

For example, it must always be a possibility that the delinquent's relationship with his mother has gone wrong at some point. If this is so, he may never have matured fully in an emotional sense. In later life, therefore, mother does not represent the loving and helpful feelings which animate a person. She may, indeed, represent only control and domination. In someone who has never been able to face up to this there may well be a lack of affection, or of the loving feeling which is needed for the making of good and warm relationships with other people. Again, it may be that a poor early relationship with father will make it most difficult at a later stage of a child's development for the child to come to terms with reasonable authority.

Ideally, a child should grow up feeling that both his parents are loving and accepting persons, yet with attributes of control and of kindly discipline, and able to include him in a secure and mainly approving family group. This security, acceptance, and approval are of

60

much importance to the proper growth of personality, but such growth may be impeded because of unconscious elements in the personalities of other members of the family.

Stott[13] has discussed in detail types of family patterns which are likely to produce delinquent members. Most of these are based on the – usually unconscious – rejection of the child by one or other parent. Basically, he examines the kinds of parental deficiency most likely to affect the child and make him delinquent. In some cases, the child's reactions to certain situations are so violent that it seems better to remove him from home. He will, Stott suggests, often react to his feelings by running away from home, or at a later stage, by wishing to take up some employment which involves leaving his parents. Sometimes it is evident that he is deliberately getting himself into trouble so that he will be sent away to some institution. Incidentally, it should be said that this kind of situation is by no means restricted to children in an apparently poor material environment, and social surroundings do not necessarily play any part in producing such behaviour.

Stott clearly and helpfully analyses situations arising from the personalities of the individual parents and their interaction, which seem to drive children into delinquency. Here we are concerned with some kinds of family group which seem in our experience to do this. No doubt there is much basic similarity between these families and those studied by Stott, but we are placing, we think, more emphasis on the situation and less on the individual parents.

The first kind of family group – all too familiar to family caseworkers – might be described as being one in which the parents are too lazy to stop the children from getting into difficulties. It has been well described in a social study by Sprott.[10] The children are allowed to do much as they like, so long as they do not get into physical danger. They are given money freely, partly because it stops them pestering the parents and partly because the parents do not see the value of any sort of control. This money relationship may often take the place of affection, which in families of this kind is frequently not demonstrated at all, or so dramatically shown that it does not ring true. Mother is naturally the parent who is most in contact with the children. She usually has no consistent standards of self-control, housekeeping methods, cooking, nor any ideas of training the children in a constructive way. Sometimes she is mentally dull, and often she will be found either at the cinema or watching the television. She will alternately scream at and caress her children or her husband. The father of the family, according to his temperament, may go out a good deal, or if he has some feeling for his home, may well be found doing a great many of the domestic chores after he comes home from work.

If he does not have much feeling for his home and family, then there is plenty of material for a 'problem family', because when he goes out in the evening he will often spend money on himself which he should have spent on the family. His wife may respond by just 'giving up', and may run up bills which will ultimately never be paid; or if she has more initiative, she may perhaps go out to work or just go out and allow the children to run riot without any form of control. In this rather extreme case the possibilities of delinquent trouble for the children are quite obvious.

All too frequently such families become, after some years, labelled as 'problem families', and the implication is that nothing can be done. They appear on the lists of all the local welfare agencies. The parents drift apart emotionally even if they remain physically together. Their children have not experienced and cannot understand any kind of consistency in approach or in discipline. Their image of parents is of people who are sometimes kindly, often violent when least expected, and altogether quite unpredictable. Consequently, these children grow up in exactly the same way – uncertain and therefore insecure and lacking in any real confidence. Sometimes they have an engaging *gamin* quality which seems to indicate confidence, but faced with any situation in which they have to rely on their own judgement, they will usually fail. Lying for them is often a perfectly normal method of getting out of trouble or getting what they want.

Although this picture is of a somewhat extreme type of family, many of these traits may be found under circumstances of much greater material comfort. In families of better 'social standing', far removed from the 'problem' label, there will be found the mother who cannot bother to give her children consistent affection, or to show them the real concern which they demand. There will also be the father who is at work all day and engaged in outside activities at week-ends and at night – the 'real good sport', for instance, who is always ready to give up his – and his family's – time for someone else. Children in these households may not exhibit the same primitive reactions because the family and neighbourhood 'tradition' does not allow it. If they do, they are seen as 'problem children'; their families are not seen as 'problem families'.

The social worker therefore must guard against a feeling that the basic emotions and relationships between members of families in different social or material circumstances are necessarily widely divergent. Whatever the family status, he must try to approach it with an unbiassed and inquiring mind, endeavouring to look below the surface for any real problems which may exist.

In families where the children are influenced by such a pattern of inconsistent and incoherent parental behaviour, it may well, at first, appear to be an impossible task to make any real change. This will especially be true of the more obvious kind of difficult family. Some social workers may tend to tackle such families in the spirit of giving material help because it seems to them that no good can be done in any other way, and also because the need appears so clear. Again, they may see the family as a challenge and rush in to try to change everything overnight. We have already made it evident that we feel these attitudes to be inadequate. There may be some necessity for material help, but unless there is also a strongly-defined attempt to give understanding, and a chance to look at the emotions behind the material problems, the purely material solution seldom succeeds.

In such families, the emotional neglect of the children is coupled with poor social and material standards, so that the children often become delinquent not only through lack of family relationships but also through lack of any real ideal of conduct or personality which they can imitate, however unconsciously. We have said earlier that even in families where social and material standards are higher, the same difficulties may be experienced by the children, and may indeed be heightened

64

because the resentment of parents in more socially conforming families may often be very strongly directed
against the children. This is perhaps because the parents
have a much keener sense of being disgraced socially by
children to whom 'everything has been given'.

The real trouble in such families is that neither parent
gives any consistent affection or pattern of behaviour.
The children consequently grow up confused, bewildered,
and without the all-important sense of belonging to a
group which values them. To quote Dr. Scott, '. . . if we
were to arrange a large sample of people according to a
scale, with those who had received consistent affectionate
maternal care at one end, passing through those who
had experienced both love and hostility from their
mother, to those at the other end who had been really
seriously deprived in this respect, then I believe that the
highest incidence of crime would be in the middle of
this scale, not at the seriously deprived end. And even
the most innocent maternal affection, if it is not comple-
mented by paternal affection, may predispose to crime –
especially in adolescence.'[21]

It is probably true that inconsistency of affection will
tend to produce instability and anxiety which may lead
to crime. But it may also be the case that those deprived
of maternal affection in particular are the more likely
to become more habitual and more violent in the crimes
they commit. Our own experience seems to show that
the relationship with father is not sufficiently emphasized,
even in Scott's statement. The whole question of the
possibility of a poor paternal relationship as a strong
factor in delinquency has been the subject of recent
research[27] and Dr Andry states, 'The role of fathers is
of great significance in the aetiology of delinquency'.

With some families, there is a continual struggle for mastery between the parents. Every opportunity is taken by one or the other to demonstrate that he or she is in control of the home. Such quarrels as arise – and they are frequent – become bitter and uncontrolled, because they often spring from deep unconscious feelings of sexual inferiority. Such quarrels are likely to be carried on when the children are present, and will be very frightening for them. This situation may produce tense and anxious children, incapable of making affectionate relationships except after a long period of gaining reassurance. Once again, it is not really possible to generalize too much, but these children may be likely to grow up emotionally disturbed rather than seriously delinquent. Their delinquency may take the form, for example, of stealing in order to give articles away so as to gain affection. For the social worker, the problem is to decide with whom he should try first of all to look at the difficulties. He may feel that the family situation is so far gone that the best hope is to concentrate entirely on the delinquent; he may undertake the attempt to resolve the parental difficulties first; or it may appear better to share the task with a colleague.

Another fairly common family situation which may result in a delinquent child arises where one parent is loving and the other either not showing affection or even being actively hostile. Some possible effects of this are shown in Chapter XIII. But there is a vast range of possible relationships between parents, even of this fairly extreme loving and hostile nature; the important point here is for the social worker to be aware of their existence and to try to look at these relationships with the family.

Where the mother is over-loving and even possessive,

our experience shows the possibility of delinquent children as comparatively likely, especially where the father is being at least outwardly strict and perhaps rather rigid in discipline. In this situation, much may depend upon the parent who is able to dominate the other. But here again the social worker will be advised to look more closely into such feelings before making any decision about long-term treatment. The strictness of the father may prove to be merely a cloak for his feeling of inadequacy: it may be due to jealousy: or it may be an ill-directed result of genuine desire to help the child – there may be great but hidden affection present. There are a variety of other possible feelings. Similarly, the social worker will need to reserve judgement on the deeper reasons for mother's attitude also. In this way, the feelings of the delinquent may be more easily looked at because of the greater knowledge of the relationships which have produced them.

Sometimes the family life may appear to be satisfactory on the surface and all seems well, yet the social worker senses uneasily that this is not so. This is perhaps a case in which the parents, though kindly and well-disposed, are not able to make really deep relationships with their children. This may on occasions be found in parents who are very intellectual. Children in such families are often over-indulged, the parents perhaps unconsciously making up for a lack of affection by a show of outward concern which the child feels is not genuine. Sometimes the child is treated as a mature individual, and receives little help with his problems. As a result he despairs of finding solutions. He takes the easy way, which can result in his living on a facile and superficial level, and becoming a complete egoist.

Social workers meet a number of families in which mother has been deserted by her husband. Sometimes she has been left to bring up the children on an inadequate maintenance allowance which has to be supplemented by National Assistance grants or by her own earnings. Some independent women make great sacrifices to go to work for this purpose: the more dependent or less competent will accept the allowance. In either case bitterness and anger is likely to be encountered, although it is not always seen at first. The possibility of the children becoming delinquent is clearly present, and the problems of relationship in such circumstances are usually very confused. It might appear at first sight that the children would be likely to have affection for mother and hatred for father. Often this seems the position on superficial inquiry. Later, however, it may be discovered that the behaviour of the parents in the marriage and the actual circumstances of its breakdown have left much deeper marks on the personalities of the children. It may be a matter of long and patient approach before any relationship with them can begin. Of recent years there has been a tendency for the effects of the 'broken home' on the children to be discounted, and statistics have been brought forward by way of proof.[6] We believe that few practising social workers will agree with the conclusions drawn from such statistics, although, obviously, many children from 'broken homes' do not become delinquent.

In any discussion of family patterns and delinquency it would be difficult to omit the people who are deprived altogether of family life from an early age. The illegitimate child, even where he or she remains with the mother, will often present special problems. Children who have been abandoned, whether through parental neglect, discord, or death, may have to be brought up in institutions or in homes other than those of their parents. However good and devoted this care may be, there remains the possibility that the child will, perhaps unconsciously, set up some barrier of feeling between himself and other people. There may later arise in his mind the question as to why his family didn't want him, or what his father or his mother were really like. He may build up some imaginary and fantastic figures of his parents, and compare them with the foster-parents he has, always to the disadvantage of the latter. Even though the explanation for his deprivation is perfectly rational, he may not be able to accept it emotionally. He may appear to accept it, but if he gets into some difficulty and a social worker tries to help him look at his problems, his feeling is often one of helpless bewilderment and bitterness, or a total withdrawal of interest in the situation.

This background of deprivation can be a persistent factor throughout life, and the deprived person who becomes a delinquent presents a major problem to the social worker. If any help can be given, it will usually be by acceptance without condemnation on the part of the social worker of a great deal of unreasoning hatred against himself and against society. In our experience the difficulty lies in securing from such people any kind of emotional response which can be used in a profitable manner.

These are some of the more common examples of situations which, we have found, produce delinquents, either as children or in later life. Let us say again that, even in the family situations we have mentioned, proportionately few people actually become delinquent. We merely say that the possibility of this occurring is greater in these instances.

We have not attempted anything like an exhaustive account of relationships within families. The rivalry of affection between children in the same family group, for example, is also a considerable factor in the growth of personality. Our object here has been to show that these feelings are the crux of emotional development and to indicate, from the groups which have been selected as examples, how some of the more difficult problems arise. The more the social worker can visualize the possible significance of these relationships in each individual case, the better will he be able to look, with the delinquent, at the way in which the present situation has arisen from them.

VIII

The Young Delinquent in School
and Community

So far we have been principally concerned with the diagnosis of delinquency and with the way in which the delinquent and his family may be treated by the social worker through a particular kind of relationship. In this present chapter we shall discuss particularly the child and the adolescent delinquent against the social background. We shall not be referring to the possibilities of treatment so much as to the importance of recognizing the need for it in the early years of the delinquent.

Let us first of all agree that the character of the immediate neighbourhood around his home must also have some influence on the delinquent. As we saw in Chapter II, the ecological theorists assert that such influences are of primary importance. Studies of neighbourhoods have been carried out in much detail, and in the one undertaken by Sprott, Jephcott and Carter[10] two almost adjoining streets in a working-class area were compared and contrasted. It was found that there were marked differences in social behaviour between the two, and particularly was this true in respect of juvenile delinquency. In the street with the greater number of children who had been before the juvenile court, many children did not regard stealing from outside their own home as being wrong. Others declared that there was no harm in stealing so long as you could 'get away with it'.

It is no news to social workers that many of their delinquent clients live in well-defined districts, especially in urban areas. But we do not consider this to be the only or even the main reason for delinquency. Only a comparatively few children in these districts become seriously delinquent. The 'environmental delinquent' as such is not usually a persistent offender as he grows up, and such areas are productive of what we have called casually delinquent people.

Nevertheless, it is always necessary for the social worker to consider the relationship existing between the delinquent and the immediate area in which he lives. Although this will be a less personalized bond than that existing in the family, it is very real. It may be that the delinquent is conforming to surroundings in which people have low standards of conduct about the law. If this is so, the aim of the social worker will be correspondingly limited at first. He will do well to realize that very powerful forces are working against any immediately successful treatment. This is not to say that treatment 'in the open' is impossible, nor that all those from such neighbourhoods should be removed from home as soon as they transgress the law. It means that the social worker must not begin by assuming that he and the delinquent will have similar standards of behaviour. He must begin with the child's standards, and not attempt to suggest different ideas until a sufficient bond of mutual confidence has been established.

In districts where delinquency is frequent, there are, of course, children who additionally lack family affection and secure relationships. Where serious emotional problems are superimposed upon a background of this kind, the difficulties of helping children 'in the open' are much increased.

In 'delinquency-producing' districts, many children are conforming to a local culture and may be quite well-adjusted to their family and their neighbours. Where this is so, unsatisfactory family relationships tend to become less easily distinguishable. But the child in an area where juvenile delinquency is unusual is a cause of concern to parents and neighbours alike. Where this happens, defects of family relationship often become evident on close inquiry, even though these again may not be immediately apparent.

On the whole, less attention seems to have been paid by sociological research to delinquents living in areas which are not delinquency-producing. The difficulties that such children have with family relationships are less easy to study because they are only made clear to social workers after much knowledge of the family, and do not appear on the surface. Children in these families are not conforming to any social pattern, but are often fighting against any conformity at all.

From his very early years, the child will absorb much from his home, his street and his neighbourhood which will influence the rest of his life. In addition, at the point in his life where he is perhaps with some difficulty beginning unconsciously to sort out these relationships, he starts school. For the next ten years at least school is to exert yet another influence upon his personality.

There is clearly an infinite variety of ways in which any particular child may react to his school life. He may accept it quite happily, and settle down throughout

73

the whole time he is at school. He may feel impelled to compensate for some inadequacy at lessons by 'showing off' inside or outside the school. He may be highly intelligent and yet somehow never be able to achieve his full potential. In other cases, some parents may have great expectations of their child which he is never able to fulfil, so that he may always have a disturbing sense of failure and inadequacy. For this reason he may more easily become liable to feelings of insecurity and anxiety which his parents may not perceive. Sometimes there may be tensions set up in his mind between home and school – for example, over homework, or over leaving school at a certain age; over dress in school and outside. A child who lives in an area where the normal pattern is to leave school as early as possible and to enter an unskilled trade will find it difficult to continue through grammar school and university in the teeth of local tradition; conversely, the boy from the ambitious home who fails to gain admission to a grammar school may carry the mark of failure on his personality throughout his life, even though he may be materially successful later on. The subject of selection for secondary education would not seem to lie within the scope of this book, but tensions may stem from a faulty placement in a secondary school which can give rise to delinquent attitudes.

The school is often the place where the child reveals openly for the first time his general attitudes, his social personality, his emotional conflicts, and his ability or inability to live with others. In addition, he shows the more obvious characteristics of intelligence level, capability in work and play, and feelings about authority. Not only will he accept or reject certain parts of what

74

the school offers, but he will also show or fail to show certain aspects of himself and his personality at school. His feelings towards teachers, for example, are often conditioned by his earlier feelings towards parents and family, and for this reason may appear quite irrational. But by the exhibition of these feelings he shows a particular and important part of his attitude towards authority itself. The teacher who is able to understand something of what is happening when he notices apparently irrational behaviour towards himself is in a better position to help the child than the teacher who takes the behaviour at its face value.

An important element in the contact of the child with the school, therefore, is his relationship with his teachers. Human nature being what it is, most teachers probably find it easier to make the friendliest contacts with those children who respond readily. Thus the child who is difficult, or who already feels unconsciously that he is an outcast, may easily come to believe that in school as in home or neighbourhood, he is not really wanted. If he rebels, the common reaction to this is impatience, for not every school has the time or the facilities to spend on difficult individuals. Even so, good teachers do try very hard to get through the emotional barrier which such children will set up. They are rewarded when they can at last perceive some response to their patience and tolerance behind the defiance, the surliness, the depression, or the indifference of the 'outsiders'. If teachers really try to understand what lies behind the behaviour of such children, it may be possible to build up a relationship between teacher and child which could make school less intolerable for the child. We have known many instances where the lively concern

75

of a teacher or of a head teacher has been of untold help to a child in avoiding a repetition of delinquency.

It is unfortunately true that in large classes only exceptional teachers will be able to find time to attempt such work with difficult individuals in school, and, except in small communities, not many class teachers can hope to have much contact with the child's home. As a result, behaviour difficulties at school and at home, which have a common basis, tend to be treated separately in each place. But the teacher can become aware of obvious behaviour difficulties at school which suggest that there are problems at home. It is here, of course, that the most valuable work of the child guidance clinic may lie, in acting as a link between home and school.

The child guidance clinic is unfortunately regarded with some reserve or even suspicion by many teachers. For this reason, its services are often, in our experience, not sought until too late. Detection of the disturbed child cannot be attempted too soon. In fact, the possibility of referring such children to the clinic should be in the mind of the health visitor who will make contact with families before the child is even of school age. Certainly teachers in primary and junior schools especially ought to be persuaded that the help of the psychologist should be sought as soon as serious problems of behaviour present themselves.

One of the most revealing of these behaviour difficulties is persistent truancy. This is nearly always indicative of some insecurity and anxiety about home. It may point to deep emotional problems, particularly in the depressed, moody, and withdrawn child. The sooner these characteristics are brought to light the more chance there will be of saving the child from unhappiness and possible delinquency later on. In these cases of persistent truancy it will often be found that the parents are not co-operative, frequently because of their own feelings about school and authority. Sometimes these parents are fined and sometimes the children are placed under the supervision of a probation officer. This seems a positive approach and is often successful. It may be possible in the future to provide a full training in social work for education welfare officers, who are frequently in direct contact with a family when the child is very young and first begins truanting. If these officers were given the training and status of family caseworkers, far more help could be given to such families at an early stage of the child's school life.

Apart from persistent truancy, there are other symptoms of emotional problems which may be observed at school. The unhappy and solitary child, for example, is likely to have such problems, and if these characteristics are noticed he is in need of help. Failure in school subjects, especially reading or arithmetic, or general lack of interest in school work; indiscipline, showing-off, and irresponsibility; resentment of school routine and restrictions; failure to join in out-of-school activities; dislike of school generally; these are each significant pointers, and if more than one is observed in the same child it may be that he also needs some help. At least consultation with parents is indicated, with the further possibility of referral to a social worker or the child guidance clinic.

Where, in addition to these symptoms, there is violence or persistent running away from home, or where it is known that the child persistently soils or

77

wets himself, expert psychological help should always be sought.

Many social workers believe that the reason that some children are discontented during the last year at school is because they feel that school is useless to them. A few will seem to have reached the limit – albeit a very low limit – of their ability to absorb any more learning, even of a vocational kind, and remain sullenly in the school doing as little as possible. Others go further and are defiant and aggressive. This type of adolescent has only one aim – to leave school at the earliest possible opportunity and to earn all the money he can.

There seems to be some evidence that puberty is now reached at an earlier age than formerly. It is possible that teachers and social workers have not yet grasped the implications of this. The material and emotional demands of boys and girls at about fourteen to sixteen years seem to be greater than they were, for instance, before the last war. Perhaps also these children have grown up in a more complex world where adult values are exhibited to them from a much earlier age than before. It may be that this is not a real but only a pseudo-maturity. Nevertheless, it is an important factor in any approach to young people of this age. Their demand to be treated as grown up may be a cause of regret to many people because it may be felt that the children are missing one of the most pleasant and valuable phases of life by growing up too quickly, but this has to be recognized and assessed.

There is, therefore, the dilemma that children are growing up faster but being retained at school compulsorily to a later age under conditions of restriction. This must be a factor of importance in creating in some children an attitude of rebellion. Indeed, the raising of the school-leaving age as recommended in the Crowther Report[28] is likely to lead – at least temporarily – to an increase in juvenile delinquency. Probably it would also have the effect of making fifteen to sixteen the peak age for children to appear before the juvenile courts.

It is often true that children who see no point in remaining at school for so long are able to make quite a surprising adjustment to life when they eventually leave and start work. If a youth of this kind finds a job with standards within his compass, he often seems to grow up suddenly. This is not only because he feels suddenly adult, but also because he is accepted as a member of a group of workmates with a less critical and demanding outlook than he found at school. He is at last earning money, and he meets congenial companions. So long as he keeps within the limits of ordinary behaviour nobody will exert much pressure upon him. There may sometimes be dangers for the future in this attitude, but the 'difficult' boy at school may develop unexpected stability and a degree of maturity in the right job.

The vast majority of adolescents, assisted by the Youth Employment Service, will go into employment in which they will achieve some balance or adjustment. But once again it is the minority who do not feel needed or accepted at work who are likely to become or to continue to be delinquents. For most people the period after leaving school is exciting and often satisfying – they have high hopes and ambitions. But for others, especially where there has been little or no feeling of security in their family group, it may be only a period of further failure to gain recognition – of drifting from job to job. Such drifting is not always through inefficiency. Sometimes it occurs through an unconscious desire to find some work or some person with whom they can feel 'safe' and not be criticized, nor have to keep too high a standard. It is not necessarily the unskilled or the unintelligent who show this inability to adjust to a milieu, and we are not including here the adolescents who change work with a genuine conviction that they are going to benefit thereby. However, Barbara Wootton says that 'all the investigators (quoted by her) are agreed that (delinquents) tend to be characterized by poor work records.'[29]

When the school-leaver begins work he enters a world which in some ways makes more demands upon him. For some who feel unwanted or insecure, this may prove too much, and this is another reason why such youths are found drifting hopelessly and aimlessly from one job to another. They unconsciously seek in their employment some element which it cannot apparently provide in sufficient measure for them – it may be the need to excel in some work for which they are manifestly unsuited, or it may be the need to find someone who will give them far more time and attention than is possible. These are the misfits of industry and commerce, who can so easily become delinquent through despair or anger at their lack of achievement.

Here again the question of relationship arises. Although normally industry has little time to sort out such misfits, occasionally there is some person at work who has the time, the tolerance, and the perceptiveness to 'get inside' them. It may be a manager or chargehand, or some workmate, or a welfare officer, but if there is someone who can see the difficulties, and has the ability to make a friendly and probably intuitive relationship, help may be given.

Many employers, not unnaturally, do not want the delinquent. This is not only because of his actual delinquency, but also because of the unsettlement and the poor school and work record which so frequently accompany it. At present this attitude is hidden by the demand for labour, but it is still there. It is of little use to minimise this problem, and there is no point in condemning employers who refuse to give a chance to someone who has been before a court. There is here, perhaps, some considerable persistence of the feeling that delinquency should be punished. Moreover, there are obviously types of work which demand a history of past honesty, and for these society will hardly tolerate the employment of a delinquent.

Not only do young people start work when they leave school, but they also enter upon a new world of leisure. Many adolescents, especially, feel a need to associate outside their homes, which may lead to friction with parents, particularly where the latter demand much of the time and attention of their sons and daughters. The widespread purchase of television sets has in some cases, where the family members are not strongly attached emotionally, tended to widen the gulf between parents and adolescents. It may be true that in many families the television set helps to keep the family together, but in others the insistence of parents upon watching the screen nightly almost to the exclusion of other activities has virtually driven out the adolescent in search of different pleasures. The television is seldom the centre of the adolescent world – this is more likely to be the record-player, and the two can easily conflict in every sense!

The school-leaver frequently has a large sum of money to devote purely to enjoyment. Wages for those between fifteen and eighteen years of age have risen strikingly since 1939, and in a much higher proportion comparatively with other age groups. The need to save money is not now so widely recognized, and from our experience a far smaller fraction of the weekly wage is demanded by parents for board and lodging. Consequently the amount of money available for the adolescent to spend on leisure activities is in the aggregate enormous. This has led to a concentrated effort by the commercial world, through advertising, to obtain the largest possible share of this money, and sometimes appeal is made to violent emotional desire.

Many attempts are made by society to help the adolescent to use his leisure constructively. The Youth Service, in the face of great difficulties, tries to do so in a particular way, and certainly has some success. Youth organizers and club leaders do look at the individual difficulties of their 'problem' members, although they are concerned mainly with groups rather than individuals. The delinquent club member is in great need of help, but in the club as everywhere else, his demands are often too great. Nevertheless, the youth worker who can spare the time and has the necessary patience and insight is in a unique position to give such assistance. Many delinquent young people have been helped to form useful and lasting bonds of understanding friendship in this way.

It will also be natural for a great part of the leisure time of any adolescent to be devoted to courtship, or at least to some form of approach to the opposite sex. We shall discuss more fully in Chapter XV the fact that the adolescent girl will not often show the same kind of delinquent behaviour as the boy. So far as the un-settled delinquent boy is concerned, his reaction to girls will usually reveal once again his uncertainty and in-security about affection, and often his demand for acceptance as well. His feelings are conditioned by his unconscious emotions about his parents and family, and as we have shown, these are frequently unsatisfactory in some serious way. Where the social worker is con-cerned with adolescent youths, he can learn much of their deeper feelings if he can encourage them to talk about their girl-friends and to discuss with him some of the ideas and feelings which they have about girls in general.

Very few delinquent adolescents we have met attend religious services, but this does not mean that they are not interested in 'religion'. They will often put forward their views on this with considerable zeal, frequently in an 'anti-establishment' way. By such discussions, the social worker will often see more clearly something of the feelings of the delinquent about parents and family. These feelings will tend to be revealed, for example, by quotation, by criticism, or by attacking the parental attitude to religion and perhaps to morals and spiritual matters in general. Many social workers will feel the need to seize this chance to put to the delinquent standards of moral behaviour or to attempt to show him something of spiritual values, and it may be that never before has the adolescent had the opportunity of such individual discussion.

Once again the better plan is to try to look with the

client at the feelings he is showing, and to wait until some understanding of these has developed before putting any moral or spiritual ideas before him.

Having looked briefly at the social milieu of the delinquent and at his possible reactions to it, we may now go on to consider the demands made by society, both on the delinquent and on the social worker. We shall see that the latter also has to understand and at times to resist pressures of different kinds which the community exerts on him.

IX

Authority and Permissiveness

An important point for the social worker to consider about each delinquent is the element of authority which enters into the relationship between them. Quite often he is in a position to exercise such authority. Even if this is not so, the delinquent may well read it into the relationship, often crediting the worker with powers he does not possess. Thus the social worker cannot pretend that authority is not there; he must come to terms with it.

We shall approach this subject by looking at various aspects of it, but first let us remind ourselves of the general attitude of the community towards authority at the present time. Broadly speaking, there is a tendency towards a relaxation in authoritative attitudes. The dangers of the harsh use of authority are widely feared. In government, in law enforcement, in industry, in education and in the family, authority is heavily circumscribed. The old-fashioned father-figure has largely disappeared from the modern 'democratic' family, and his counterpart in other spheres of society has been similarly dethroned.

Together with this development has come anxiety about 'rejecting' the delinquent. It may be that in our modern Western society there is greater tolerance for the delinquent than in any other. This fear about the use of authority, coupled with anxiety about rejecting the delinquent, has led to an uncertainty among parents as to how they should manage their children.

This kind of uncertainty has spread in our society, and the social worker has not escaped its effects. If this development can lead to careful thought followed by wise action, its results may be advantageous in the long run.

The work of August Aichhorn is worth studying in relation to the problem of the wise use of authority with delinquents.[30] Working with a small group of aggressive young hooligans, he carried permissive tolerance to the ultimate degree. The boys, living together in a hut, were allowed to do exactly what they liked. Their most extreme hostility and violence was met by a consistent friendliness and kindness. In the beginning, this attitude was interpreted as weakness, and consequently aggression and destruction were rampant. After a time, however, the boys' behaviour improved and they were able to accept, gradually, a training regimen which eventually re-educated them into useful citizens. 'Permissive' institutions of this pattern have since been successfully developed.

On the other hand, establishments such as the average approved school, with an authoritarian structure, also have their successes. Permissiveness seems to achieve good results, but so also does the firm use of authority. Perhaps one of the explanations of this paradox is that in both types of school, concern for and interest in the children are plainly shown. But this may not be quite the whole story. Michael Burn, in his brilliant account of the work of G. A. Lyward at his school for maladjusted boys at Finchden Manor,[31] illustrates how Lyward has different expectations for different individuals. He uses discipline and permissiveness in varying degrees with each boy. There is something here for the social worker. He too may use his authority differently and to a different extent with each delinquent he meets. Although he cannot possibly be permissive in the same way as could Aichhorn in his very special circumstances, he may perhaps find it easier than Lyward to vary his treatment of individuals in the open.

Thus he may demand from one youth, where he thinks it necessary, a higher standard of punctuality, regularity of attendance at interviews, good manners and smartness of appearance, than he does from another. Some will be capable of sustaining a long conversation, whilst for others five minutes in the social worker's room without uneasiness will be an achievement. The social worker must be sensitive at all times to the delinquent's needs and capacities. He must try to judge the mixture of authority and permissiveness needed in each relationship, ensuring that what he expects from, and permits in each delinquent is consistent with the reasonable expectations of society.

It is perhaps the aggressive, hostile teenager who presents the greatest problem. It is he who may require the maximum toleration from social workers. In this way he may be enabled to come to terms with his anger against authority and with his deeper anger against one or both of his parents. At the same time the community cannot be expected to suffer too much aggression. The dilemma for social workers is a very acute one. Even the most experienced among them will find that in some cases there is no satisfactory solution. Institutional treatment is sometimes imposed, not because it is the best form of treatment but because the community can be tolerant no more and must have protection from the delinquent.

On the other hand, there are delinquents who, whether or not they are fully conscious of it, have a great need to be controlled. The use of authority here by the social worker is of great value. He is the 'line-drawer'; he marks the limits of acceptable behaviour. Consistent firmness with such cases is the supreme virtue – bearing in mind that the delinquent's contact with the social worker must end one day, so that a tapering-off or weaning process is eventually required.

Most delinquents come somewhere between these two extremes. We spoke earlier of the delicate balance in each social worker – delinquent relationship and we reiterate it here. The ultimate aim of the social worker in this may be put in general terms. He will strive to develop a situation in which the delinquent is able to accept reasonable authority, direction, and discipline. If a helpful relationship grows up between social worker and delinquent, the chances, even with quite an aggressive young man, are hopeful; for if he can come to terms with an authority represented by the social worker, then he may come to accept authority when he meets it in other forms, so long as he understands the need for it.

With the younger delinquent, the use of authority or permissiveness by the social worker may lead to disagreement or even conflict with the parents. The parents may expect the social worker to support them in their strictness, or they may expect him to be severe where they have been weak. On the other hand, they may resent the social worker demanding more from their child than they do themselves. Each situation will have its own peculiarities. The social worker should not seek disputes, but he should not shrink from trying to find the reasons for parental attitudes, even though the attempt may produce hostility. In any case, the social worker must take care not to succumb to parental pressure against his own judgement.

For instance, some parents have been greatly disturbed by their adolescent sons wearing Teddy-boy clothes. They read into this and into the adoption of succeeding fashions a delinquent attitude to society which may not necessarily exist. If they involve the social worker in supporting their condemnation of the clothes, he can easily find himself in a welter of anger and recrimination which will militate against any helping relationship and which will take him far away from the attempt to understand and explain underlying causes.

Sometimes, in our rapidly changing society, the older social modes, some of which are enshrined in statute, may seem to have become outmoded. This can put the younger generation out of sympathy with their elders, and vice versa. The age at which young people should smoke, be served with cigarettes, get married, or have the vote, are points upon which there is this kind of disagreement. In an age of automation, industry is not such an obvious virtue; nor is thrift, in a society which enjoys national insurance against sickness and old age and whose economy is increasingly dependent upon hire-purchase. Rapid social changes mean that the adolescent is preparing, perhaps half-unconsciously, for life in a world which his parents do not fully understand.

We touch on these matters to emphasize the danger of the social worker becoming too caught up in the battle between the generations. If he is too firmly attached to one side, he may find that the help he can give in self-understanding and in mutual understanding is negatived.

Let us consider an example. The parents of a sixteen-year-old girl come to the social worker for help. Their daughter, they say, is contemptuous of them, and seems to despise them. She will not help in the house, or come in at night when she is told. She will not tell them who her friends are, or talk about anything she does.

How should the social worker handle the situation? Women social workers usually find in this type of case that the girl is quite willing to accept a friendly invitation to talk things over. The aim of the social worker, as always, will be to develop a relationship in which the girl will feel able to discuss her feelings. It need hardly be said that the social worker should be sufficiently youthful in outlook and take sufficient care about her appearance for the girl to feel that they can 'talk the same language'; yet at the same time she should not pretend to be 'one of the girls'.

It may be that the girl has rather over-restrictive parents, who for one reason or another try to impose rigid standards of behaviour. 'They want me in at ten o'clock every night, so that I can never stay to the end of the film,' the girl tells the social worker. 'All my friends can stay out until eleven. I do help in the house, but Mum never thinks I do enough.'

It is perhaps easy in this sort of situation for the inexperienced social worker to over-play the 'permissive mother' role. She identifies herself to some extent with the girl, sees things largely through her eyes, seems to make an excellent relationship with her and encourages her to stand up for her apparently reasonable rights. She may even tell the parents how silly they are being. This may sometimes work, but more often than not, it doesn't. It may well reduce the parents to indignant impotence, lead the girl on to a quite exaggerated assertion of her demands and widen the breach in the family. It could even – perhaps the ultimate disaster as the parents would see it – result in an illegitimate child. Of course the girl's motivations may be deeper and more involved than this, and we shall be discussing the subject more fully in a later chapter. Our object at present is to see how the social worker, at a simple level, can do better. Probably the most useful role for her to take in relation to the girl is that of an adult who is friendly and interested but who is not afraid of exercising authority where necessary. She should normally show sympathy and concern but at the same time be prepared to show firmly where the necessary lines are to be drawn. This 'line-drawing' in fact emphasizes her concern. She may work with the parents, in the hope of helping them to come face to face with their need to be stricter than other parents, but all the time she must let the girl see that she (the social worker) is not *for* or *against* the parents.

As we suggested in Chapter VI, through the developing relationship with both girl and parents the social worker may sometimes be able to explain one to the other. As well as trying to help them to understand themselves, she may also attempt to help them to understand each other. She can perhaps explain the girl's feelings to the parents and the parents' feelings to the girl better than the parties involved may ever be able to do. So long as she does not appear to be taking sides or taking the girl away from her parents, her intervention may be effective. It must be said that the preservation of this balance is not an easy matter.

Where the parents of an adolescent are inclined to be harsh, they may not always be susceptible to change in attitude, or the social worker may not have much opportunity for influencing them. Provided, however, that he takes care not to undermine the basic loyalty of the young person towards his parents, the social worker can do much on quite a superficial level. His friendship and his reasonably tolerant, understanding attitude can be very helpful in steering the individual concerned towards emotional maturity without an outright revolt against his parents. In some cases, it may be possible to help the boy or girl concerned to understand more of his situation and the underlying causes for his need to rebel so violently.

In situations where the parents are weak, vacillating and ineffective, it may be more helpful for the social worker to play a different role. Here it may be necessary for him to represent the sterner aspects of authority. The strict, consistent disciplinarian is a particularly easy – sometimes a deceptively easy – role for the probation officer to play; so too for the schoolmaster who attempts a social-worker approach with some of his pupils. It fits in with the expectations of the public – and often of the delinquent himself. Consistent, reasonable firmness is the essence of what is required in such cases and sometimes it is effective.

If the case is to be dealt with intensively, however, the ultimate aim will be to help the parents themselves to understand a little of their own difficulty in exercising authority. Because of this, care must be taken not to undermine such confidence as the parents have. An encouraging and supportive role, initially at least, pays dividends as far as this is concerned. Later on, in some cases, it may be possible to assist one or both parents to see their own behaviour and attitudes more clearly. The father, for example, may be able to talk to the social worker about his early memories and his hostile feelings towards his own very stern father. It may be that eventually, with the help of the social worker, he may be able to come to terms with the fear of losing his child's love by correction or punishment which is at the root of his weakness.

The parents who say: 'We've given him everything he's ever wanted but still he gets into trouble,' may be the despair of the magistrates, but they can be helped considerably towards a readjustment of their attitudes if the social worker has the opportunity of making a successful relationship with them. Change, if it comes, should be gradual; it should be akin to growth. Very rapid swings in parental attitude, either towards discipline or towards tolerance, can lead to unhappy consequences. This is partly because such change is not founded on truly established feelings and partly because the delinquent himself is not prepared for it.

Implicit in the discussion of the proper use of authority is the recognition that the social worker must himself have come to terms with authority. He must be able to accept it where necessary himself, must be at ease in representing it and imposing it where the situation demands, but be able to refrain from using it when it would be unhelpful. If he has reached this stage in his professional development – and it implies some considerable degree of maturity – then the way is open for him to learn to use it effectively within each relationship he makes. But the use of authority will only be of lasting value and effectiveness to the extent that the client understands, and genuinely accepts, his need for it.

X

The Social Worker's Feelings

The relationship between the social worker and the delinquent has been described as 'professional friendship'.[32] We hope we have already made it clear that this is something different from ordinary friendship. In this chapter we shall talk about some of the feelings of the social worker, so let us begin by discussing how his relationship with the delinquent, while akin to ordinary friendship, differs from it.

Perhaps the first difference is that an ordinary friendship is frequently made without very much reflection. Most of us seem to make friendships to meet our various and changing needs, which may be partly or wholly unconscious. The relationship with the delinquent, however, is usually made deliberately, for a certain definite purpose.

Within limits, both parties to an ordinary friendship are able to enjoy their emotional satisfactions without too much thought for the effect upon one another. In his relationship with the delinquent, however, the social worker ought not to indulge his own emotions. He may quite rightly derive satisfaction from improvement in the delinquent, but that is as far as he should legitimately go. He will not, for example, use the delinquent as a confidant or as a refuge from his own loneliness, or as someone who will gratify his need to be depended upon – that is to say, he will not do it wittingly. Like other human beings, he will have unconscious needs which he will satisfy through his work. It will be for his colleagues to help him to understand some of these. None of us can be expected to know ourselves fully, and perhaps the most that can be asked is that we should try to be aware of this possibility.

Again, in an ordinary friendship both parties may normally be expected to express their feelings spontaneously. They usually have no great need to weigh very carefully what they are saying. The social worker, in his relationship with the delinquent, will often have to consider with care the words he uses. He must think carefully too about the emotions behind those words.

Furthermore, the social worker strives, as he does not in ordinary friendships, to be conscious of something at least of what is going on beneath the surface of the relationship. He is not omniscient and there is much that he will miss, but he tries to understand his own feelings as well as those of the delinquent. In addition, with varying degrees of success, he tries to control his feelings and the responses they engender in him.

It follows from this that, ideally, the social worker is in some sort of control of the situation. His aim is consciously to help the delinquent by using the relationship which is developing between them. This is so, however simple his purpose. The relationship between them is not the end in itself, as is normal with ordinary friendships. It is a means to an end.

It may be thought that in saying all this we are straying into the ideal world. Some readers may already be thinking to themselves that no social worker can be as detached and cold-blooded as we imply, nor can he be so omniscient. With this we agree, and put our argument no higher than to say that if the social worker is (as he should be) the sort of person who can put warmth and feeling into his relationships, then these will be more useful and no less genuine because he has attempted to gain some insight into them.

It is important to realize that much feeling is usually aroused in a relationship of any depth, although for various reasons this may quite often be well concealed. This feeling is two-way: from social worker to delinquent and from delinquent to social worker. In order to understand a little more of this, let us imagine a social worker sitting in a room face to face with a delinquent he is trying to help, and let us reflect upon the sort of emotions he may experience.

First of all there will be feelings about the delinquent and his offence which are right on the surface of the social worker's mind, and of which he is immediately conscious. Supposing the delinquent has exposed himself to a young girl. If the social worker has a young daughter, his feelings may be different from those he would experience if he had not. If it were his own daughter against whom the offence was directed, his feelings would be different again. Such feelings are part of the situation and must be taken into account by the social worker.

The delinquent's appearance, demeanour and general situation may cause the social worker to react in a certain way. He may feel pity, for example, or impatience, contempt, boredom, envy or protectiveness. It is relatively easy to make oneself conscious of these immediate feelings the delinquent arouses, and it is also helpful, because it may indicate the sort of feelings he arouses in others.

The social worker must be careful, because these feelings may not always be objective. We all carry with us some of the prejudices of our family, our class, our sex or our nationality. These prejudices can colour our attitude to the delinquent and it is not an easy matter to be aware of them. For example, supposing the social worker believes in thrift and the delinquent does not. If he automatically assumes that thrift is a virtue, then the delinquent's thriftlessness may make him very indignant. He might think that anyone would be indignant, when in fact a colleague might not. It could be that his indignation is disproportionate and that he is expecting more from the delinquent than the latter can give.

His beliefs about the nature of the world and man's destiny in it, and about right and wrong; his religious or moral tenets; these are naturally of fundamental importance to the social worker. He is entitled to his own beliefs and standards, but he is wise if he does not apply them to other people. The delinquent is usually at loggerheads with the reasonable demands of society. The social worker may be able to help him to understand why this is so and perhaps enable him to move towards a readjustment of attitudes, but all the time the social worker must try to deal with the delinquent as he is and not as the worker would like him to be. The adjustments must be those which come naturally to the delinquent and which are as far as possible reconciled to his present view of life. Change, if it is to come, must come from within: it cannot be imposed. We make no apology for repeating this, since it is one of the main elements of 'treatment in the open'.

The social worker may have ideas about the setting

in which he works, and about the operation of the law. It is very helpful for him to be aware of these ideas, and they are all part of the reality in which his relationship with the delinquent is developing. A social worker may, for instance, think that the law in certain ways is misguided. This view is bound to influence his feelings in his relationship with someone who has broken that particular law. At the extreme, if he felt that the entire machinery of trial and punishment was wrong or foolish, then his whole attitude to delinquents and their behaviour would be coloured by this opinion.

The more, therefore, that he knows about his own feelings in regard to the behaviour of others the better. He should be particularly interested in his own 'dislikes'. Sometimes these are traits in himself which he hates and represses, and he then feels especially angry about them when he sees them in other people. Whatever their basis, it is important to try to know them and not let them affect the relationship with the delinquent. There is considerable difficulty if some type of offence, such as homosexuality, physical violence, or sexual promiscuity, especially arouses his indignation. The trouble is that some at least of the delinquent's behaviour is thought reprehensible by most people, so that it is hard to distinguish between normal dislike of it and irrational condemnation.

None of this means that the social worker must become inhuman and discard all his standards of conduct, or give up all normal emotions. It means simply that in his professional relationship with the delinquent he must always be trying to look a little more closely at himself than he does in his ordinary private life.

As the social worker sits talking to the delinquent,

some of his feelings may not really stem from the current situation at all. They may derive from earlier relationships which in some way are similar. Something of this will also be seen in our discussion of the delinquent's feelings, but if it seems a strange idea, it may be useful to reflect upon the feelings that some people have when they are interviewing a headmaster. Boyhood experiences may colour the whole interview, although they no longer have any real relevance to the present situation. In a similar way, the social worker may treat the delinquent as though he were his own son, and do this quite unconsciously.

The mature person in any relationship is usually able to grasp the situation at a fairly early stage and deal with it realistically, but it is well to repeat yet again that there are these unconscious emotions in ourselves which we bring into all our relationships. No person can know what is unconscious, but by means of discussions with colleagues experienced in this kind of advisory and consultative work, it is possible to gain some insight into the particular sort of reaction which the social worker may have to different persons and situations.

As he talks to the delinquent the social worker will probably be conscious of a wish to help him. It may be that it was this wish to be of help to other people which originally led him into this kind of work. It is a valuable driving force, but it presents certain dangers. The need to feel a 'good' person is occasionally overwhelming. It can lead the social worker to make superhuman efforts on behalf of his client, but if he feels that he must be the only 'good' person in the other person's life, then the client's freedom to develop his own 'goodness' may be inhibited. It is very hard for anyone to change himself

99

by his own efforts, but it does help if it can be realized that people can have this kind of feeling in relation to others.

The social worker may be imbued entirely with this wish to help. Even if this is so, loving feelings are not the only ones he will experience for the delinquent during the course of their relationship. On the part of the delinquent, loving or friendly feelings may not be uppermost at all. With delinquents more than with any other kind of person, a hostile phase is commonly encountered, often early in the relationship. This hostility – it can sometimes be called hatred – may be clearly and obviously demonstrated, or it can be sensed, for example, from sulky silences, missed appointments, or unpunctuality. The social worker's feelings about this hostility are of importance.

One of the most valuable attributes the social worker can develop is the capacity to tolerate this hostility – not just temporarily, but, if necessary, for some considerable period. By tolerating hostility we mean not responding to it in an immediately instinctive way, for example, by indignation, fear, recrimination, depression or withdrawal. There are some people who cannot bear any kind of angry or hostile feeling directed against them. One sees this in parents who cannot control or correct their children, because they fear to lose their children's love. If there are social workers who feel like this towards their clients, they will find work with delinquents particularly difficult. Naturally, the social worker's capacity for tolerating hostility varies with each individual. Whatever the capacity, however, it can be extended enormously by the effort to understand himself and his attitudes.

There are some people, social workers among them, who seem unable to recognize hostility when they encounter it. It is hard for some to admit that anyone does not like them, with the result that they do not 'see' the dislike. If the social worker is going to be able to develop an effective relationship with the delinquent, it is important that he should school himself to see the 'negative' as well as the 'positive' emotions engendered. We shall be discussing this subject again in Chapter XVI.

From recognizing hostility, it is a logical step to consider the acceptance of failure. In working with delinquents, failures are so obvious when they occur that they cannot be ignored. Sometimes they are unexpected; at other times the social worker is not surprised when he finds the delinquent in further trouble. He must learn to accept his failures without being too discouraged.

On the other hand, society will usually place the blame for the breakdown entirely upon the delinquent and tend to regard the social worker as someone who has been frustrated in a praiseworthy attempt to help another person. But the good social worker must see further than this, and try to examine each case in order to recognize his part, if any, in the failure. If he can do this with sincerity and honesty, he can grow in experience and in knowledge of his own strengths and weaknesses. In this way lies the development of professional skill.

To be over self-critical, though, is unhelpful. However conscientious and gifted the social worker may be, he is not a divinity ordering the destinies of others. He is a very ordinary human person, entering into a simple human relationship. Mistakes and errors of judgement will certainly come his way. If he can learn not to brood upon these and to realize that he can never be solely responsible for the destiny of those he is trying to help, he may then more easily use not only his errors but his successes as stepping-stones to greater understanding of the work he is doing.

XI

Attitudes and Pressures

One of the important reasons for considering the feelings of the social worker in his relationship with the delinquent is that, in one way or another, these feelings will affect his attitudes in each interview and thus colour the entire relationship.

We concluded the last chapter by urging the social worker to see himself as an ordinary person entering into simple human relationships. If he can do this, he is relieved of considerable strain, since he does not demand too much of himself in the production of miraculous results. Many beginners in social work find themselves tongue-tied in their first interview. This is usually because they want to do too much. Their inexperience makes them feel inadequate to their high purpose and thus they are anxious. This anxiety is revealed in tenseness and strain.

Lack of tension derives from the absence of anxiety. The social worker can be free from anxiety if he has sufficient knowledge of himself, is not too critically conscious of his own shortcomings, and has realistically limited aims. However, the 'if' is quite a big one. Experience is important, but even the beginner can go a long way towards relaxation in the emotional sense if he tries to concentrate not on his own needs but on the needs of his client.

A lack of tension is epitomized by naturalness, which

in this sense does not mean the free expression of one's emotions, but rather easiness and poise. Sometimes a person is described as 'so delightfully natural', and this is indeed a delightful trait. The social worker who is natural in this way is free to display a genuine concern without over-emphasis.

Concern is a word we have used already in indicating the social worker's proper attitude to his client. Although horror or contempt are clearly unhelpful, the plain man might be excused if he asked whether sternness would not be more effective than concern. It is obviously impossible to state exactly what attitude will be most helpful in every case, but it can be said that although the social worker cannot hope to like every client, he does his best work with those he does like. Concern for the client in the sense in which we are using it means caring about him. It is basic to all effective help for the delinquent in the open. Although the worker can give some help to those he does not like, he can seldom give any to those he does not care about at all.

There are some people who have feelings for others but cannot show them. Social workers often meet so-called affectionless mothers. These may sometimes be women who for some reason are unable to demonstrate their love, whatever feelings they may experience. If love is not demonstrated to a child so that it can realize that the emotion exists, then that child may feel, quite naturally, that love is lacking altogether. It is the same with the delinquent. It is not sufficient for the social worker to feel concern: it is vital to let the delinquent realize its presence.

There is no magic about this concern. To most of those who take up social work it comes naturally, because they are interested in other people and want to help them. If natural interest and desire to help is not disturbed by excessive anxiety, then it will come through in the interview well enough. There are social workers who are over-anxious about their clients just as there are people in all walks of life who are over-anxious about their work. This is not helpful, and should not be confused with the feeling of concern described above. The deep unconscious origin of this concern need not enter into this present discussion, although we acknowledge its presence and its possible importance.

It is often asked whether it would not be more effective to be stern with delinquents and show them where they have gone wrong. This can certainly be helpful sometimes. Sternness and criticism do not necessarily conflict with this attitude of concern. Just as a strict father may still be a loving father, so, in some instances, sternness and criticism in the social worker's attitude may serve to emphasize the concern he feels. But to be effective, such an attitude, as we said earlier, must be deliberate and not merely an instinctive reaction. In addition, it must be acceptable to the delinquent, in the sense that he must be emotionally capable of 'taking' it. If he is not, then a sternly critical line may be very damaging to the relationship.

Sternness and criticism run contrary to an attitude to the delinquent which has been urged by social workers in the United States and is described as 'non-judgemental'. It may be asked how anyone can be expected to be non-judgemental with delinquents. Where they have been before a court, society will have judged them already. If they have not made a court appearance, the parents or relatives and others close to them will have judged them. The social worker can hardly help reflecting some of this judging. 'Non-critical' is equally unsatisfactory, since, as we have suggested, criticism can indicate concern. 'Non-condemnatory', although less mellifluous, is probably the nearest description of the attitude. The social worker no doubt condemns what the delinquent has done, but he need not condemn the delinquent himself. Rather, he accepts the delinquent for what he is and thus accepts all his bad feelings – hostility, aggression, deceitfulness, selfishness, childishness or whatever they are. Accepting the delinquent as he is, the social worker is able, if the delinquent is willing, to look with him at the good parts of his nature which seem to have become submerged.

This may sound theoretical but it has been proved in practice to be the way to begin. Probation officers have found, for example, when preparing a social background report for the court, that apart from other considerations, a deeper, more helpful relationship can eventually be achieved if they present to the court the bad as well as the good side of the delinquent's personality and behaviour. The explanation of this probably lies in the unconscious sense of relief the delinquent experiences at meeting someone who sees and yet tolerates the bad parts of his personality which to others, and often indeed to himself, are so intolerable.

The conception of acceptance is, however, easily misunderstood. It can be confused with condonation. Condonation can seldom help a delinquent, but, unfortunately, it is a form of emotional collusion into which even the most experienced social workers can at times unwittingly slip. We shall be looking at this more closely in later chapters.

So far, then, the social worker is seen – and how ideal he must appear! – without tension, composed and natural, feeling and conveying concern, accepting without condoning his client's bad feelings and behaviour. What more can be expected of him? Or rather, what further targets can he be encouraged to aim at? Patience, of course; this follows logically from what has gone before, as does consistency also, since no attitude is likely to be effective if the client cannot rely within reason upon it not changing in essentials. The fact that some delinquents will 'try-out' the social worker, in order to see if in fact his attitude will alter or fluctuate, is quickly learnt. Far harder to learn is not to dance to the tune of the client's emotional piping.

No one should assume from what has been said that perfection lies in the social worker; he is as human as anyone else. The attitudes we have suggested are ideals for him to achieve where he can. What may be expected is that he will come to know the sort of approach which may be helpful, but will be wise to acknowledge that he will be unable always to follow it as he would wish.

We would also like to emphasize that the social worker in showing concern is not committed to a continual expression of approval. It may be that approval of achievement, as discussed in Chapter IV, plays a major part in some cases, but it is only one element in the total attitude of concern.

Inherent in all that has been said so far is the idea that the social worker's attitudes should be engendered by his conception of the delinquent's need and not by his own instinctive response to the emotional pressures upon him, wherever these originate. For the delinquent is not the only source of pressure upon the social worker. The community generally has expectations as to what he should be and how he should behave. The expectations of the community in respect to an education welfare officer, for example, may be expressed through the local education committee. The committee will expect results: it will expect children to attend school regularly. This is a very real pressure, since such results are what the officer is paid to produce. Further, if the committee feels that its officer should not be 'soft' with truants, the pressure upon him to be 'tough' is direct and strong. Even if the committee itself has no expressed views, the pressure of community opinion towards those concerned with school attendance can have a powerful influence, though the officer himself may not be fully conscious of it.

Again, if the community expects advice-giving or moral didacticism or religious exhortation from its social workers, the individual worker may find himself at least a little uneasy in withstanding such expectations. Occasionally, a social worker is led to accept entirely the role apparently required of him. If people continually ask for his advice and defer to his opinion, then he may come to feel that he should be able to solve all their problems. This assumption of an 'oracle role' is made quite unwittingly. His clients may expect a lot of him, but they do not usually expect omniscience: it is he who feels that these demands must be met. There is no need to emphasize that he is placed in quite a false position. His assumed omniscience makes it more difficult for him to offer real help to his clients, whilst they in turn are retarded from learning to solve their own problems if they are encouraged to look to him to do this for them.

A pressure sometimes even more immediate than the

delinquent's or the community's expectations arises from the expectations of the delinquent's family, should he have one. We discussed some situations of this kind in Chapter IX. These expectations may range from the clearly discernible attitude of the parent who says 'I want you to give my daughter a good talking-to', to the more subtle sympathy aroused by the apparently pitiable condition of a drunkard's wife.

Let us take the first example; does the social worker administer the 'good talking-to' when asked? The beginner may find it hard to resist, especially when the parent is standing waiting for him to do so. The more experienced worker will realize at once that by agreeing he is demonstrating quite clearly whose side he is on, and possibly thereby losing all hope of effecting any readjustment of attitude between parent and daughter. This straightforward pressure, often expressed in the 'You're too hard on him' or 'I don't think you're strict enough with him' type of remark, is more easy to resist than the more devious approaches. What does the social worker feel as he listens to the widowed mother's recital of the wrongs her seventeen-year-old son is inflicting on her? 'He won't wash up a cup, he won't dig the garden, he won't even go to the shops for me. He says he hates his little brother and he wishes I'd died instead of his dad.' The pressure here, usually not directly expressed, is for the social worker to go and *do* something with the boy, to tell him how badly he is behaving and to *make* him be kind and helpful to his mother. This unconsciously subtle appeal to the social worker's instinctive pity can, if he is not careful, lead him to accept everything that the mother tells him, and by agreeing with her, confirm her in her attitude to her son. This may preclude him later from attempting to help her to look at the possessive nature of her love, and to understand the unconscious demand to make the boy meet some of the emotional needs previously satisfied by her husband.

None of this must be interpreted as meaning that the social worker should ignore the family's emotional pressures. On the contrary, he is asked to be especially sensitive to them. But sensitiveness does not mean compliance. He must think about what appears to be expected of him and try to see the underlying feelings. Often he will fail because the pressure is too sudden and immediate or too subtle and hard to see.

We mentioned a drunkard's wife. It must be accepted that in cases where a woman is married to an alcoholic and the marriage is of long standing, there may be a form of unconscious collusion between husband and wife. Unconsciously, the wife wants her husband as he is, although consciously she does not recognize this. As she details day-to-day trials and humiliations, the social worker may feel under tremendous pressure to change things – perhaps to help her get away from her husband. If he complies with this pressure, he will often find his efforts strangely resisted, not only by the husband but by the wife. Cures are very difficult and medical help is usually necessary. A beginning may be made by helping the wife to reach some sort of understanding of her unconscious needs. This cannot be done if the social worker reacts instinctively to the superficial emotional pressures of the first interview.

It must not be thought that we are suggesting that the social worker is likely to be impervious to all the different and sometimes conflicting expectations which impinge upon him. He is, we repeat, a human being, and like other human beings is inevitably susceptible to the spoken and unspoken demands and feelings of his fellows, of which he may not always be fully or immediately conscious. Some pressures arise directly out of the setting in which he works and he cannot ignore or resist them. The education welfare officer, as we have seen, must see that children go to school, the N.S.P.C.C. inspector cannot permit cruelty to children, the probation officer must try to enforce the requirement in a probation order that the probationer live honestly and industriously. Over and above such 'setting-pressures' are those which stem from the social worker's own conception of his function, from the community, from his client and from his client's family. These, we have seen, are varied and often not immediately obvious. The hope is that the more the social worker knows of the kind of emotional pressures which exist, the more reflective and realistic will be his response to them. That he can begin to recognize them and, if necessary and practicable, resist them, is a mark of his professional development.

XII

The Teacher and the Delinquent

In Chapter VIII we looked generally at some of the child's attitudes to school, with particular reference to the feelings of the delinquent child. We can now consider how the school and the individual teacher may help the delinquent. Much that we have said already about the social worker's approach may be applied directly by teachers, but there are situations worthy of discussion which arise specifically in schools.

As experienced teachers already know, not all children who pose a problem of discipline at one stage or another in school are likely to develop into delinquents. Adjustment to society does not necessarily imply a rigid conformity and neither does a satisfactory adjustment to school. Those who present a disciplinary problem may be discussed in terms of 'normal' and 'abnormal' conformity. The 'abnormal non-conformer' is the potential delinquent; the 'normal non-conformer' is not. Prominent among 'abnormal non-conformers' is the child who is maladjusted and who seems to work out his disturbed feelings upon his fellows rather than within himself. Central to this category would be the delinquent gang-leader. Such social adjustment as he can achieve is in a group in opposition to society and to the school.

It should not be assumed, on the other hand, that the child who gives no trouble is necessarily well-adjusted. It may be that the passive 'conformer' is in fact potentially delinquent. He may even be severely maladjusted, but, because he suffers within himself, this is not immediately apparent. Although his behaviour suggests anything but delinquency, he may nevertheless one day break out. Even if he is never delinquent, it may be found that in later life he is quite inadequate to play his part in the adult world.

In our consideration of the roots of delinquent behaviour, we talked of feelings of anxiety and insecurity engendered initially within the family and its relationships. We saw that the delinquent or the potentially delinquent child may bring such feelings with him into the school setting. If such a child commits delinquent acts, it is likely that the simple disciplinary techniques – the 'social controls' discussed in Chapter IV – will be ineffective or only partially effective. Thus the teacher who relies entirely upon them, whatever his success with the normal child, will fail with the delinquent.

It must be recognized that some schools fail with delinquents where others succeed. In those that fail, the head-teacher's attitude, if not that of his staff, will often be that his school is not equipped to handle delinquents. His duty, he will feel, lies with the normal, non-delinquent majority. He will say that he wants the work of the school as a whole to improve, and consequently, he must remove disturbing influences. There are special schools for delinquents, he will add, and it is to these that offenders should be sent.

Head-teachers with these views may go on to justify their attitude of rejection by implying that the delinquent is beyond redemption, because he has a bad streak, or comes from a poor home, or never was any good. This viewpoint is unfortunate, since a helpful school with understanding teachers can do much to assist some delinquents to develop more acceptable attitudes and behaviour. Any disadvantage to other pupils is outweighed by considerable benefit to the community.

It will be generally agreed that it is the attitude to delinquents of the head-teacher that usually sets the pattern for the rest of the school. The head, himself, can be considerably helped if he has readily available the services of the educational psychologist. It is he who can give the head the support, and sometimes the confidence to persevere, which is often needed.

We discussed in Chapter VIII some of the signs by which the teacher may recognize the child in need of special help. To assist teachers in this and also to help them to decide if the difficulties can be eased within the framework of normal school life or whether skilled psychiatric treatment is required, Dr Stott has devised a questionnaire.[33] By completing this for each child, indications of unsettlement become apparent. There is always a danger of such rule-of-thumb methods leading to children being wrongly and unfairly 'typed', but if it is used wisely, the questionnaire can be most helpful.

If a delinquent is to be helped at school, nearly everything depends upon the attitude of the teacher towards him. If the teacher can see the delinquent's conduct in its true light – as reflecting, more often than not, an emotional handicap every bit as real as a physical one – then he will be mentally poised not to react to it in a rejecting way. Many delinquent children unconsciously provoke rejection by being deliberately and obviously difficult. If such a response is provoked in the teacher, then the delinquent feels even more certain that he is unlovable and lacking in worth, and that he is justified in his unloving attitude to others.

If the teacher is not to react instinctively by punishing and rejecting, how then should he deal with the delinquent? We mentioned in Chapter IX how G. A. Lyward, at his school for maladjusted children, treats different children differently, tolerating behaviour in one that he would not permit in another. Something of this approach is demanded of any teacher. The aim, as we have stressed, is to create an atmosphere in which the delinquent can feel secure and in which he can achieve something which will be thought worthwhile. It may be said that a tolerant response to the difficult child creates problems of favouritism. If he is not punished, or if he is praised for some trivial achievement, then other children will expect similar treatment. There is some truth in this, but less than seems apparent at first. Children are not always envious of the extra indulgence or attention extended to the unhappy, disorientated child. They often recognize that he is 'different'. They are not so likely to see it as favouritism as they would if an obviously well-behaved, successful child were involved.

In school, as elsewhere, it is easier to recognize the delinquent than to deal with him. Yet dealing with him need not always involve great difficulties. An understanding attitude from the teacher and the creation of a secure atmosphere is sometimes enough. But the school in which the delinquent is set apart, derided before others, or criticized by members of the staff, has no hope of doing other than make the situation worse. Most teachers would recognize this today. The rejection of the delinquent, however, can be more subtle. Some teachers unconsciously reject emotionally the less satisfactory pupils. They may not criticize them, but they never give them praise, or provide an opportunity for simple achievements.

As an example of a case in which such a simple achievement was praised, we may cite Mary. She was a tall, weak-looking girl, subject to illness of nervous origin. Her mother watched over her to an almost pathological degree, and even when Mary was quite fit it was difficult to persuade her mother to send her to school. She eventually appeared before the juvenile court, having failed to attend school without good reason, and was placed under the supervision of a probation officer. After a time she did begin to go to school occasionally. Co-operation between the probation officer and the headmistress was good, and one day Mary came to see the officer in a state of great delight. She could hardly wait to explain that she had today received the first good conduct mark in her experience at school – for having completed a whole week's attendance without any absences. This would be taken for granted in the case of most children, but in Mary's case it was not normal, but an achievement of much merit in view of her difficulties, and was recognized as such by the understanding headmistress. Although this did not solve the problem, it meant a great deal to the girl and her attendance improved somewhat.

Earlier in the book, we talked of possible unconscious reactions in the social worker to the offence itself. These apply equally to the teacher, but there are attitudes to offences which are peculiar to the school setting. A recent UNESCO Report[34] illustrates this well. It considers three offences: a boy steals pennies from his mother, a pen from a class-mate and a bicycle from the street. All three are thefts, but the teacher sees each of them in a different light. The first is of least importance to him because it does not affect the school. The second is of more consequence because it happened in school. The third is even more serious because the police will take action and public attention will be focused upon the school. It is obvious how irrelevant these reactions are in terms of fundamental delinquency and yet they are not so uncommon as to be exceptional. Again, the identity of the offender may influence the teacher's attitude. He may well regard the offence with greater abhorrence if committed by a 'bad' pupil, than if it was done by one of his best scholars. Such attitudes are most important. They may literally tip the balance in some cases between delinquency and a reasonable adjustment to school life. The school with a real sense of duty to the community will not reject its delinquents nor measure their acts by the way they reflect upon the school. Rather, it will feel concern for them and some responsibility for their behaviour.

When a pupil is to come before a court, the most helpful attitude is for the head-teacher, while giving accurate facts in his report, to remember the offender's good points. If he feels he possibly can, he should ask the court to permit the offender to return to the school. Should the court find itself able to do this, the offender may be impressed by the fact that his school tried to help him when he was in trouble. This could be the reassurance of concern and acceptance which he is seeking, and it may be the beginning of better things. Some head teachers discuss such reports (before presentation) with the delinquent and perhaps with the parents also.

A child who has been dealt with at court should not

usually be punished at school as well. Many delinquents, as we have seen, feel much shame, although they often cannot or will not show it. Some, indeed, feel that they are so bad as to be quite unlovable. Such children are on the look-out for rejection, and find it in even slight criticism, let alone further punishment. It only needs one or two members of the school staff to comment on the court appearance for them to feel that everyone is against them, and their adjustment to the school and to society is made correspondingly more difficult.

Admirable though the facilities of the newer schools often are, they may mark out the socially maladjusted delinquent and engender in him a feeling of rejection. Where the provision of a gymnasium and a shower-bath carries the need for clean clothing and towels, the child from the less satisfactory home stands out, and realizes that he stands out. Again, the frequent striving for higher academic standards militates against the unsettled child. So much of the interest and attention of the teacher goes to the child whose home background gives encouragement to academic achievement that there may be little left for those who could be helped so much by it.

It may be asked if the school must always confine its efforts to the individual delinquent, or whether work with parents can be attempted. It is unhappily true that the parents most in need of help have the least contact with the school. Thus, active work with parents, except where a probation officer or other social worker is concerned in the case, must await the fuller development of a service of trained school welfare officers. In the meantime, there is much that the school may do to promote a more helpful relationship with the homes of its pupils. Mutual understanding seems to be the key. Even where this is not possible, the school can always seek to understand the home backgrounds of its pupils. The grammar-school boy from a rough working-class background, for example, is most vulnerable to social pressure from outside the school, and is in particular need of the sympathetic help of his teachers. This can only arise from an understanding of his position.

We can best conclude this chapter by putting the situation in perspective. Seriously delinquent children form only a tiny minority of the pupils in our schools, and the schools cannot hope to solve completely the problems even of this small number. There will always be a proportion of delinquents who will not respond to help offered by the school – or indeed by anybody else. Furthermore, the teacher has a primary duty towards the 'normal' majority, and he must not neglect this. We accept all this, and are yet convinced that the teacher has a considerable and sometimes vital part to play in the efforts of society to deal with its delinquents. Finally, we are certain that this part can be played most effectively if teachers and particularly head-teachers can understand the delinquent as an individual with special problems of relationship, and with hidden feelings of insecurity and lack of acceptance such as those we have outlined here.

XIII

The Delinquent and his Offence

We are now able to consider in greater detail the delinquent in relation to the offence he has committed. Dr Glover has pointed out that the legal classification of offences gives no indication of their psychological origins,[35] but nevertheless certain types of offence seem to be loosely associated with certain personality developments and certain family situations. These in turn point to particular methods of approach and may sometimes indicate the relative prospects of successful help.

There are offences, for example, which seem to indicate an unconscious attempt by the delinquent to prove his manhood. Whether or not they involve violence, they will certainly contain an element of daring and aggression. Quite often the delinquent concerned comes from an over-protective family, and he is likely to have an over-loving mother who smothers him with her affection and is often working out her own unconscious problems to an inordinate degree. The taking and driving away of motor-cars is a common offence of the teen-age male, and often the urge to do it stems from such a situation. With a minority of offenders this may be repeated in a compulsive way.

The fight to settle unconscious doubts about his manliness usually subsides as the youth becomes a man, but sometimes it can harden into a life-pattern. The authors know of one delinquent who, after 'doing' a detention centre and a Borstal institution, went on to join the French Foreign Legion, impelled by such an urge.

An offence which presents difficult features for the social worker is that of stealing from the parents. When confronted by this, one usually looks at once to the delinquent's emotional feeling about the family. Frequently this type of offence is associated with rejection, real or fancied, by one or both of the parents; often, though not invariably, by the mother. It sometimes seems to be a result of worry about an earlier separation from the parents, which seemed to the delinquent like rejection. In this situation, he is often 'testing-out' his parents as we mentioned earlier, to see how far love for him really does exist.

Stealing from the family gas or electricity meter by a teenage youth – it is uncommon in girls – is recognized by probation officers as frequently involving such feelings. In its true light as an offence directed against the parents which is certain to be discovered, it is likely to represent something more than the desire to acquire a small amount of money.

Quite often, persistent and apparently purposeless pilfering similarly indicates some unconscious feeling about rejection. Such thefts frequently begin with stealing from mother's purse, later extending to other people's property. Children seem to begin their lives with an unconscious feeling that they have an inalienable right to parental love. If they do not receive this, or if they believe themselves deprived of it, one form of reaction may be delinquency.

The affectionless character is said by Bowlby,[14],[15] to be the result of severe maternal deprivation. Such a person presents a considerable difficulty to the social worker. The help that is offered is through a relationship, but the affectionless character is unable to make or sustain a relationship. Child care officers in particular are familiar with this sort of person. Apparently anticipating rejection in every human contact, he goes out of his way to get it. Bowlby suggests that such a person has been deprived of mother-love at an early age. Where he is removed from his own family, his history is frequently one of movement from one mother-substitute to another, because he is unable to accept love and unable to give it. His offences often seem purposeless, but they are usually frequent and are often aimed against people who are trying to help him. He frequently becomes an inmate of an institution, be it Children's Home or Approved School, and as he grows up, presents the typical picture of an institutionalized person – withdrawn, friendless, unable to tolerate ordinary frustrations and unable to make normal relationships. The situation is very sad and the social worker will feel he must do all he can to help such a person. Persistent friendliness coupled with consistent firmness may possibly meet with success eventually, but the worker should not be surprised at failure. The modern trend towards the creation of smaller institutions may do something to help such people. Where inmates and staff are few enough for all of them to know each other well, the development of a satisfying relationship may be possible.

Some offences are committed in gangs, and the gang is a normal phenomenon in the development of adolescent youths. It affords among other things companionship and the support of a close, approving, group. It is a means to emotional growth in that it facilitates for many the development of independence from the family circle. An offence committed with a gang would thus usually argue a more normal attitude in the delinquent than would one committed alone. The adolescent is characteristically insecure and uncertain, and it may be surmised that this applies strongly to gang-members, especially if they are not found among the leaders. Generalization is difficult because in some communities membership of a gang is so much part of the accepted social pattern that a youth is abnormal if he is not a member. However, membership of a gang specially directed to delinquency may indicate serious anti-social tendencies.[36] Whether there is more violence in our society than there used to be is a moot point. Certainly more offences of violence are being dealt with by the courts. Most of these offences are gang phenomena. Gang fights are sometimes part of the accepted social behaviour of an area – in the poorer parts of some of our large cities for example. But not all violence is due to social influences alone. Some of the worst examples of violent crime seem to stem from early parental rejection which has developed a fierce aggressiveness in the person concerned. Such a person is difficult to help because he provokes and assaults others so violently that society demands protection from him. A more hopeful aggressive delinquent from the social worker's point of view is the one whose upbringing, while not altogether without love, has involved severe and frequent physical punishment, quite often inconsistent and unpredictable. Such a youth may tend to behave like his parents, but he can be influenced by a social worker if he is fortunate enough to come into contact with one at the right time. Club leaders, particularly if they are of the athletic type, are well-placed to help.

123

Hooliganism involving wanton damage and destruction is a common activity of the delinquent gang. It is usually public property that is attacked – trees and flowers in parks, street lamps and shelters for example. These are readily available and inadequately protected. There seems little definite distinction between the teenage male hooligan and other delinquents of his age. He is usually, but not always, from the working-class, and often from a group which is unhappy and resistant in the last year at school, or unsatisfied in employment. He may have an antipathy to authority or to the entire adult world. Certainly he will enjoy the security of the gang and the excitement of its destructive – and usually nocturnal – activities. If the social worker can win his liking and respect, it may be possible to redirect him towards a more constructive use of his energies. Wanton damage is normally characteristic of a certain phase of development and most young people may eventually be expected to out-grow it. Those who are more fundamentally delinquent are likely to turn to other kinds of offence.

Indecent exposure is an offence which is viewed with a mixture of pity and disgust by the general public. The offender is commonly thought by one half of the community to be in need of medical treatment, and by the other half to merit punishment. The feeling shown by this offence is one of unconscious aggression and seems to be connected with a desire to show off a masculinity which the offender does not really feel he possesses. Although the large majority of social workers confronted by the need to help this kind of youth seek psychiatric or medical help for him almost as a matter of course, it is often not helpful for the offender to think of himself as a chronic medical or psychiatric case. In youths, the offence seems to be part of an unsuccessful attempt to cope with the upsurge of sexual feelings, and may have been committed quite frequently before it is brought to light. Offenders are often rather shy and withdrawn people who are not able to make normal approaches to girls of their own age. They occasionally have parents who tend to be inhibited sexually, and we have frequently found the family situation to be one in which the father is unassertive and retiring, and mother is dominating.

The adult exhibitionist is a different matter. His offence may have become a form of compulsion, and he is then in urgent need of psychiatric help. But however much he may protest his wish to be helped, there seems to be a part of the really confirmed exhibitionist that feels such pleasure in the act that he does not want to be cured. Such an unconscious attitude makes pscho-therapy most difficult. But where the offence is an isolated one, committed perhaps at a time of illness, emotional stress, or family trouble, the intervention of a social worker with acceptance and insight is likely to be helpful.

Clearly, in a single chapter we cannot hope to deal with every possible offence, but it is worth mentioning the confidence trickster, who is often a persistent liar. This condition seems to stem in many cases from an un-satisfactory relationship with the father. The offender often seems to have a sense of inadequacy, due perhaps to his feeling that he has never had his father's liking, respect, or regard. In dealing with such people, the social worker will often be amazed at the way in which they persist in a falsehood up to the very moment of the inevitable discovery of the truth. It is frequently found that the falsehood seems to be of no apparent advantage to the offender at all. If the social worker is to succeed with such cases, he needs to have considerable self-confidence and skill. The situation is greatly helped if the delinquent has a wife who can help him in a slow weaning from his fantasy world. Steady and persistent confrontation with fact in opposition to this fantasy is part of the treatment. But it is not easy to make the strong and deep relationship which is essential to any real progress. Some confidence tricksters seem to be able to sense intuitively the weaknesses of their victims. Intelligent, quite hard-headed people are persuaded to part with their money in a way that astonishes them afterwards. This is widely known, but it is worth emphasizing in order that the social worker may be forewarned. He must be prepared in advance, so that he himself is not so influenced. To collude, as it were, by becoming a victim himself is obviously quite fatal to any helpful work.

Social workers find it difficult to help tramps for reasons briefly referred to in Chapter VI. Such men (tramps are rarely women) do not stay for long enough in one place to make any real, continuous contact with another person. Haphazard welfare provision relieves a situation temporarily, but achieves nothing permanent. Compulsive travelling, with all its attendant disadvantages in our settled society, usually indicates quite a severe instability. There is often a history of a severely disturbed childhood and antipathy to the father. The condition is difficult to influence and the social worker is well-advised not to set his sights too high. As we said earlier, it is better to let the tramp make his own plans and for the social worker to confine his efforts to listening, giving moral support, and supplying material needs if he really considers it wise.

Homosexual people are sometimes referred for help to social workers. A distinction should be made between those who have at one time experienced heterosexual feelings and those who have not. The former may have fallen into temptation but be anxious to revert to a heterosexual outlook if only they could do so. The confirmed homosexual, although he may be unhappy and depressed, does not usually have any real wish to be different. He has no drive to change himself. It may be that the social worker can sometimes help him adjust to his circumstances and condition, giving him support in his efforts to construct a satisfying life without coming into conflict with the law. It is more difficult with homosexuals than with other offenders to make any sort of general suggestions, not only because of the moral issues involved but also because of the tangle of possible origins and objects. Edward Glover has discussed the deeper motivations of homosexuality and shown some of the emotional conflicts which seem to produce it.[35] Psychiatric diagnosis is always indicated, but treatment can be helpful only to the man who has a genuine wish to change his sexual attitudes – and the wish, though genuine on the surface, may be impossible to fulfil because of unconscious conflict.

The offence of arson seems to be symptomatic of a prolongation into adulthood of feelings of emotional deprivation. It is no easy matter for the social worker to achieve a good relationship with a person who feels like this, but it can sometimes be done. It has been found that painting of a very colourful kind is helpful. So far as the feelings of the social worker are concerned he will need the ability to live with anxiety, because he may sometimes feel that the person he is trying to help is in certain moods a danger to the community.

In children, the urge to play with matches and light fires, if persistent despite warnings and punishment, is often symptomatic of a feeling that mother has withdrawn her love and interest. It may be that mother cannot show her real feelings, or she may be too ill or too preoccupied to give the child the demonstrated love it needs. Where this fascination with fire exists it can be surmised that the child unconsciously interprets the situation as one of emotional rejection on the part of the mother. Many children display neurotic traits at one time or another, however, and the situation generally is quite hopeful if the social worker is able to help the mother to readjust in some measure her attitudes or patterns of living. Alternatively it may be possible for the father to be encouraged to give the child in some ways a part of the love and interest it is unable to get from its mother; although this may not be the best solution, under some circumstances it may be the only possible one to try.

Among the hard core of confirmed criminals will be found the forger, the safe-breaker, and the pickpocket. These professional criminals usually have an ingrained hostility to society. They are a minority, but they constitute a severe problem. In the present state of knowledge it must be recognized that the hopes of successfully treating such people are small. However, probation officers have discovered that sometimes – usually in middle-age – some apparently confirmed criminals reach a point where they want to stop their criminal life. Contact with a social worker at this psychological moment may occasionally result in unexpected success.

Some research has been done on this question of relating types of offences with types of offenders,[37],[38] but much more is needed. Until it is forthcoming, the social worker is compelled to work from his limited and inevitably incomplete experience. We have only tried to indicate briefly possible explanations, and have not attempted to enter into any deeper motivations. Certainly, it should not be thought that our generalizations are rigid and invariable. Our main object has been to suggest to social workers that the offence itself is a clue to the personality of the offender and to his emotional attitudes. We shall be happy if we stimulate further study of the subject.

XIV

Approach to the Delinquent

In earlier chapters we have tried to show in very simple terms something of the delinquent's state of mind. We can now look further into the matter of approach. By this we mean the attempt to weigh up the feelings involved and the possibilities existing at the beginning of the relationship between the delinquent and the social worker.

One of the first things to be considered is the feeling of the client about what he has done. In approaching this the social worker may be presented with a mass of irrelevant excuses or recriminations by the delinquent, his family, and his associates. The actual offence is of much importance because it may give the first clue to the personality or problems of the offender. The worker is naturally led to look at the underlying feelings and attitudes, some of which have been discussed already. He must estimate what the behaviour means to the delinquent himself, and what emotional or other forces have led him to do whatever he has done.

Some regard should be paid to the possible feeling of confusion which may exist in the mind of the delinquent, especially if he is appearing in court. He may feel that the court and all its powers are arrayed against him. He is frequently terrified of the Press and publicity. He does not understand the proceedings. The whole majesty of the Law seems to him to be focused on his punishment.

As a result, quite apart from any deeper feelings, the delinquent may be expected to be confused and apprehensive, so that he will not easily understand that a social worker, such as a probation officer, can want to help him, simply because he associates the probation officer with the court and the atmosphere of punishment as he sees it. Such feelings must be considered by the social worker in any approach he makes.

It must be remarked at this point that it is quite common to discover that a person detected in some delinquent act may cease in the future to offend again in the same way. However, because the emotional problems underlying the act itself were never satisfactorily resolved nor, perhaps, even suspected, he thrusts them as far as he can out of his mind. The result is that later on they may recur in different forms, perhaps in some neurotic manifestation. On the other hand, with some, commission of further illegal acts may be inevitable before there is any alleviation of their difficulties, but this the law or the social conscience may not condone. The probation officer, for instance, can be placed in a dilemma when a person on probation offends again. The officer may rightly feel that the delinquent will respond to further leniency on the part of the court, but the court has to consider the welfare of society as a whole. Social workers generally may consider the offender as of more importance than the offence, but the law frequently will not.

First, then, what does the offender himself feel about his immediate situation? Is he genuinely worried by his position and concerned about repeating his offence, or is he simply afraid of punishment? The social worker must try to estimate whether there is basic insecurity and fear:

whether bitterness and resentment are present. Perhaps the delinquent is saying, in effect, 'Lots of people do this – why pick on me?' He may be able to give some reason for committing the offence, but this should usually be regarded with caution because he will often have had time to produce some rationalization, perhaps being unable or unwilling to express the real feelings which prompted his delinquency. In fact it will be found in many cases that his understanding of his motives is confused or entirely absent, and this may become something which the social worker may take up later when a useful relationship has developed.

In the second place, what does he feel about himself? Does the social worker perceive at all clearly any of the feelings in the delinquent suggested in previous chapters, such as insecurity, hostility, aggression, or rejection? If so, he will more quickly be able to pick up some of the possible causes, and see if the feeling can be related to family or other origins. Often these emotional bases are not obvious and will take much time to discover. This time is not in any way wasted. In fact, it will frequently happen that the social worker will find that even the attempt to seek such feelings is a new experience to the delinquent. It may be the first time that anyone has made such an effort. His parents and family may have failed to give him that amount of attention and interest; indeed, this lack of interest may in itself be one of the roots of his problem. His delinquency may represent to him some sort of reaction against a real or fancied lack of affection for him in his family, and his own inability to secure for himself a place of importance in the group.

As the relationship between the social worker and the delinquent develops, the former will be observing his client's feelings towards him. In the early stages, for instance, suspicion may be dominant; later this may be replaced by dawning confidence or friendly response – or it may be replaced by anger or resentment. Any reaction sensed by the social worker is of importance, and its recognition and development is helpful to an effective use of the relationship, even though it may at first be a negative one – that is, one in which hostility, anger, suspicion, rejection, fear, and 'negative' feelings of this kind are dominant.

Apart from the client's feelings about himself, his situation, and the social worker, his attitude to his whole environment must be taken into account. This will include his feelings about his work and his leisure, about his friends and acquaintances, about his schooling, and any other factors which he may bring forward in early interviews, and which seem in any way important.

It may now be helpful to look at some of the reactions of more specific types of delinquent whom the social worker is likely to meet, and so illustrate some of the underlying emotions which may produce them. For example, the boastful and aggressive type of young man is commonly found amongst delinquents. He is the centre of trouble in the youth club, the obstacle in the path of the teacher's work in school, and the one who asks for his cards as soon as he is reproved at work. It is, of course, possible to meet this conduct in a similarly aggressive manner, but this does not really attempt to solve his personal problems. As a rule it seems only to confirm his anti-social attitude. Perhaps punishment can be combined with help. Temporary exclusion from the club, for instance, may be coupled with an attempt to look at the real problems he is hiding, which will show him society's disapproval of his actions but not give him the chance to feel cast out and unwanted, because interest in him is still being maintained.

In dealing with most delinquents, the first consideration of social workers is that somewhere in the family at some time a relationship has failed to develop or developed unsatisfactorily. In the aggressive exhibitionist youth the urge to show off may cover up the feeling that he has not been accepted in some way by his parents or his family. In order to prove his worth he has to make it plain that he is more daring or better in some way than his friends or acquaintances – usually in an anti-social way. He feels that as a person he is not good enough to be accepted simply for his own qualities. This is not difficult to understand, but it provides a lead for the social worker to follow in any attempt to help. It may prove only guesswork – it may not be a correct lead, but it is a start, and if it fails, other leads may be taken up and followed with more advantage later.

Although this may serve as a general assessment, it cannot as a rule be put to the client directly, or early in the association. It is therefore better to have some initial aim in the approach to the delinquent. Often with a youth of this kind it may be helpful if he is allowed to talk as much as he will, so as to see what is brought out in his conversation and what is concealed. He will usually talk at first, apparently superficially, about his leisure activities, his likes and dislikes among films or dance-bands, his taste in clothes; later may come criticism of work or authority (which probably at this stage includes the social worker) – these and many other topics will help to build up a picture of the client's personality, from his own point of view, and not so much from the social worker's. Very probably he will continue his exhibitions of daring, for example by making a noise whilst waiting to be seen, or by being actively rude or discourteous in conversation.

Here also the personality of the social worker becomes of much importance. Is the worker able to accept this kind of childish and immature behaviour? Does he feel impelled to meet it with a rejoinder – very humanly! – about trying to behave decently for the sake of the youth's parents, or his future, or something of this nature? This may prevent the making of a relationship at once, unless it is done with the very object of provoking further exhibitions of the same kind so that they can be taken up and discussed later with the delinquent.

As discussions continue, the social worker will have to decide whether any special matter is brought forward in them with more urgency or feeling, or even more frequently, than others, and this will obviously be the best point at which to begin any attempt to look at what the client is feeling apart from what he is saying.

As an example of these aggressive exhibitionist people, we may take the case of Jack. He had been before the court for stealing and was placed on probation. In the early interviews he was aggressively cheerful, very noisy in the waiting-room, and yet he came regularly and promptly. In a short time he was telling the probation officer that he, Jack, would soon be buying a car – not a little Ford, like the probation officer had, but a Jaguar. Jack explained that he had no time for small cars. At the time he had just started work at eight pounds a week and was in debt to the extent of about £60. Later he said that he would swim the Channel within the next three years. Soon after this he was boasting of the conquests he could make of the opposite sex. All this was listened to, and eventually the probation officer said he wondered why Jack told him about the future rather than about the present. He got a vague reply at first, and for the next two interviews Jack again talked in the same vein. 'You don't need to worry about me,' he said, 'I know where I'm going – I'll be rich in a few years.' The probation officer said he wondered when Jack was going to start all these things, and who would help him and stand by him – perhaps he would take all his present friends into this world of riches with him?

In the next interview Jack began to show some worry – he didn't think he had many friends anyway. After this, he quite suddenly talked at length about his unhappy childhood, the divorce of his parents, and his experiences with foster-parents. In fact, he was able to show himself as a frightened, deprived, and lonely person. Now the probation officer could begin to help him, in so far as it was possible to do so, by looking at some of the realities of his present life, and the bitterness and resentment which were producing his fantastic ideas. Luckily, he started work at about this time with an understanding type of employer, and also got lodgings with a landlady who was prepared to tolerate many of his vagaries. The fact that he had been able to bring some of his real anxieties and fears to another person who did not laugh at him or condemn him, but accepted his bad features as well as his good ones whilst offering some help in explaining his problems, was of tremendous assistance to Jack. He no longer felt the need to show off so much, and although he will never be a strong and forceful personality, he can more easily cope with life at his own level.

Some people are tense and openly anxious, and frequently show signs of physical distress such as trembling, sweating, continual swallowing, and have pallid features. Ordinary reassurance does not usually give them much help; the client has first to be assisted to talk in a useful manner. People of this kind, once encouraged, may talk at great length but say very little of importance; indeed it seems that they are putting up a barrier or defence against any show of real feeling by talking. The social worker will probably see fairly quickly the confusion and distress which is present, and instead of trying to reassure by denying its existence, he is probably better advised to interrupt the flow of talk with some relevant question relating to the confusion or worry itself. Perhaps from this may emerge some of the more pressing problems which can then be tackled singly.

Another almost obsessionally talkative type of client may be the one who at first seems to need to control the situation. Often it is difficult to see any possibility of interrupting such people without appearing restrictive. It may, however, be helpful for the social worker to bear in mind that to many people of this kind, outside control from another person comes as a definite relief. Their acceptance of it may be surprisingly swift and they may show real progress in the relationship. Control of discussion may imply control of feeling, and this may be their greatest need. It may be that the delinquent has never before encountered anyone who realized this, and attempted it in an understanding way. As we have remarked earlier, the social worker will meet many delinquent people who will be helped not only by control of this kind, but also by the imposition of limits of behaviour and discipline. They will often accept these, somewhat unexpectedly, when they feel really secure in their relationship with the social worker.

It sometimes happens that a delinquent person becomes as it were too securely attached emotionally to a social worker, and difficulty may then arise in ending what has become a situation of dependence. This can best be done gradually – in a practical way, by lengthening the period between meetings and progressively making the meetings of shorter duration; and in other ways, by encouraging the client to venture ideas and opinions, by provoking argument, and of course, best of all if it is possible, by showing the client how the dependent feeling has arisen. Sometimes it may be a good plan to state a definite date for the conclusion of the interviews and to adhere to this date, whatever happens. This should be borne in mind, for example, towards the end of a period of probation or other supervision.

A client who remains silent can drive some workers to despair. It sometimes seems that a worker can get nowhere at all with a person who cannot bring into discussion anything at all of himself. The barrier may, of course, be added to by the social worker himself, who consciously or unconsciously may find this kind of person almost intolerable. This very inability to communicate may be the best thing to concentrate upon during the initial stages of the relationship. Sometimes the social worker will judge that it is better to remain silent himself, if he senses the atmosphere to be relaxed, and the silence does not raise too much emotional pressure in his own feelings. Eventually some starting-point has to be found, and a direct question such as 'I wonder why neither of us can talk much?' may be productive. But if both client and social worker do sit for long periods in silence, it may be possible to discuss eventually what is happening to the feelings of both in this situation. Here the crucial questions for the social worker are 'What does this silence mean to my client, to me, and to the feelings between us?' 'Are these feelings indicative of underlying hostility, of security, or something else?' and 'How can the delinquent be brought to discuss them?'

It is of course possible that a silent person of this kind is withdrawn because of some serious emotional disturbance. He may live in a world of fantasy, so that it may not be possible to reach his real feelings at all. He may eventually be able to talk about his hobbies, his daily round, his activities, but never about himself or his ιeelings. It may be that he is terrified of allowing anyone to suspect how bad he feels himself to be, and that this attitude is a defence of his inmost personality. The person who exhibits these symptoms will not easily allow himself to be changed in any way. Very skilled treatment is necessary, beyond the ability of the ordinary social worker.

If a relationship does not develop which the worker feels to be satisfactory, this may be due to the complexity of the delinquent's personality. Perhaps he is too inhibited or 'shut-in' to allow anyone to involve him in this way. Social workers are sometimes inclined to feel that the reason lies in their own inability to get through to a client, but in this type of situation self-criticism is not always appropriate. However, if a worker finds that difficulties always seem to arise between himself and clients of a particular kind, he might be wise to consider whether the barrier is not on his side, and look for possible reasons. This is the sort of self-examination, mentioned in Chapter XI, which can lead to useful results.

The few examples described in this chapter may at least show the social worker some possible lines of approach to the delinquent. There will in most cases be a mixture of many reactions on both sides which will need much sifting out.

To sum up, the social worker must be alive to even trivial indications, must not accept the surface situation but look for the problems beneath, and must seek an atmosphere in which confidence can be given and mutual understanding achieved. He must try to comprehend the delinquent's feelings as well as his own and to look at the interaction between them. This interaction forms a large part of what we have called the relationship. Such a relationship cannot be achieved by words alone, and the personal sympathy and intuition of the social worker will also come into play. If the worker can let the delinquent feel accepted, needed, valued, and loved for his own qualities, and make him able to accept some control and discipline because he himself feels the need for these, then the worker is well on the way to doing the most that he can for his client.

XV

The Female Delinquent

In this chapter we shall discuss the main forms of delinquent conduct which seem more peculiar to girls and women. It would seem that there are at least four distinctive kinds. First, of children brought before the juvenile courts as beyond parental control or as being in need of care or protection under the Children and Young Persons Act of 1933, girls predominate. Second, the neglectful mother is more in evidence, though not necessarily more in number, then the neglectful father. Third, shoplifting is a feminine crime more than a masculine one. Finally, there is the prostitute.

Females of any age group are far less likely to appear in a court than are their male counterparts. Morris[8] suggests that this is because 'resistances to delinquency are greater amongst girls: not only are they more strictly brought up, but they tend to approach sexual maturity more quickly (than boys)'. He thinks it possible that the dull and backward girl is more prone to delinquency because of her immaturity and impulsiveness. Stott[12] says 'Whereas girls may choose [*sic*] different forms of breakdown or delinquency, their anxieties are basically the same (as their brothers').' Gibbens says of girls, 'Waywardness may replace delinquency in those for whom stealing represents a substitute for affection'.[39]

Girls are brought up in the same family or social environment as their brothers. If they are less involved in delinquent activities it seems to be because the emotions expressed in such activities in males take different forms in females. Certainly, females generally seem more individualistic but less blatantly anti-social or against authority. It is, however, worthy of notice that there has been during recent years quite an appreciable increase in the number of females appearing before the courts, and for such apparently unfeminine offences as housebreaking or robbery with violence.[40]

Bovet[11] comments upon this difference in the proportion of girls and boys who come before the courts, and says that in later life more adult women than men voluntarily attend psychiatric clinics. He concludes that 'if the girls are less delinquent . . . it is not because their inner mental equilibrium is better . . . But the anomalies of mental development in girls jar less upon society than those of boys. Girls are less aggressive, their difficulties take forms which are considered, wrongly, to be normal female traits, and for this reason are more easily tolerated.' He goes on to show that examples of neurotic behaviour in girls are not easily recognized, therefore not treated, and lead later to disorders in the mental equilibrium of the adult woman. He adds 'When this neurotic adult woman becomes a mother, her children will suffer from her difficulties, and . . . if they are boys they may show manifestly anti-social behaviour, even delinquency.'

This idea is of considerable importance to the social worker who tries to help the delinquent, since it confirms that he must seek the genesis of the delinquency in the family relationships.

The Criminal Statistics for 1959[40] show that 3,253 orders were made in cases of girls before the juvenile courts as being in need of care or protection or beyond the control of their parents. The number of girls of juvenile court age who were found guilty of actual offences, both indictable and non-indictable, was 6,085. 35 per cent of the total number was therefore made up of girls who had been brought before the courts without necessarily having committed any offence of a criminal nature. The comparable figure for boys is 1.66 per cent, which reveals a most remarkable disparity.

Barbara Wootton[29] has much to say on the subject of the small proportion of females to males appearing before the courts. She suggests that such explanations as that put forward by Sir Basil Henriques based on the premise that 'boys seem to express their unhappiness by delinquent acts, girls seem to find an outlet for theirs in sex' are mythical. But she does not mention the remarkable figures in our previous paragraph. These would seem to show that waywardness almost as much as delinquency brings girls into court. It is also true that a higher standard of 'moral' behaviour seems to be demanded from girls and women than from boys and men, even at the present time. Many parents are more frightened if they believe that their daughters are likely to be seduced than they are of their sons becoming seducers. The illegitimate child and the early forced marriage may after all be the feminine equivalent of masculine delinquency. It is probable that the same emotional factors operate in both male and female, but for some reason not yet understood the males are overtly delinquent in much greater numbers.

Although adolescents are now more independent, both economically and socially, than they have been for a considerable time, legislation in England has not so far recognized this. Many young people are able to leave home and maintain themselves soon after leaving school. But if they do this before they are seventeen their parents may bring them before a juvenile court as being beyond control. Parental consent to marriage under the age of twenty-one is still required. The age of consent by a female to sexual intercourse is sixteen. The latest age at which a young person may appear before a juvenile court is the seventeenth birthday, but he or she will attend the youth employment office until eighteen years of age, and may enlist the help of the children's officer also up to that age.

A case which illustrates the confusion that exists in society and in individuals over this matter of responsibility and maturity is that of Belinda. She was fifteen years and eleven months old when she was brought before the magistrates by her parents, on the advice of a woman police constable. It seemed evident that she was beyond the control of her parents. Belinda had been warned for frequenting a café which was notorious for its clientèle of young men of very doubtful reputation. She had been there several times very late at night, and indeed the father felt it necessary to bring her before the magistrates because she eventually remained in the café all night. Her parents told the court that they could do nothing with her. She was placed in a remand home after she had been found to be in need of help, so that the necessary inquiries might be made. The subsequent medical report stated that she was not *virgo intacta*. She was of fair intelligence and 'anxious to go home and make a fresh start'. Her school report said that she had done quite well at her school but had become resistant to authority during her last year there.

The probation officer found her a pleasant girl, but

feeling confused and angry about her parents and family. She resented the attempts of her father to impose upon her the same discipline that she had been content to accept when she was younger. Moreover, she felt that she ought to have more freedom than her two younger sisters aged fourteen and eleven. Belinda had also formed a strong attachment for a young man aged nineteen, and did not wish to give up seeing him. She said that she would do so, however, if she could return home.

Father was a man of forty, rigid in outlook, angry with Belinda for forcing him to go to court, and unable to understand why his attempt to impose a discipline of a regimented kind had failed. He insisted that she give up the young man if she were to return home. Mother, a small, worried-looking woman who worked all day at a local store, seemed unable to come to any decisions of her own. It began to seem that Belinda had received little real affection from either parent. Certainly she herself felt very much alone in the family.

The magistrates made a supervision order, and the probation officer decided to work both with Belinda and her family. She interviewed the girl alone every fortnight and with her parents in the intermediate weeks. Her aim was first of all to explore the relationships in the family and to see whether Belinda's parents could be brought to express more overtly any affection which they might have for the girl.

During the next few months Belinda tried very hard. She got work in a local factory and she liked it because the girls and women accepted her and she them. She felt one of a friendly group. Belinda made a good relationship with the probation officer and was able to talk about the resentment she had felt towards her parents even when she was much younger, because she was sure they favoured her sisters and 'left her out in the cold'. She talked about Arthur, the young man against whom her father was so bitter, and explained that she felt he seemed to need her affection as she needed his.

With her father, however, little success seemed possible. He could not see that he might be mistaken in his attitude towards Belinda. His own parents, he said, had been strict with him – many a good hiding he got from both of them, and it had done him good. The probation officer tried to look with him at his deeper feelings about this, but before any change was possible, Belinda left home and went into lodgings. Her mother, who had lost both parents at an early age, rather surprised the probation officer by encouraging the girl to do this. Belinda took the step because she wanted to resume going with Arthur, and felt she ought not to do it furtively. She discussed the move with the probation officer, who was doubtful as to its wisdom but felt it better to let the girl decide. Belinda was by now nearly seventeen, earning enough to be independent of her parents financially, and much more understanding of her own problems as well as those of her parents. She married Arthur with the consent of the court and with her mother's approval and they settled down apparently quite well. Father, still seeing the probation officer, began after the marriage to see something of his own needs for giving and receiving affection, and came to more understanding of his children. Through this the two younger daughters achieved a more tolerant and helpful relationship with him than Belinda had been able to make.

Here the factors for producing in a boy some open

delinquency were very evident. With Belinda, they produced a rebellion against her parents by 'disgracing' a respectable middle-class family in another way. The probation officer, working largely upon the needs the girl had for affection and to be 'wanted' for her good qualities, was able to fulfil these to some extent and to enable Belinda to feel more grown-up, mature, and responsible.

Of the problems often encountered in adult women, those presented by the neglectful mother are usually of difficulty to the social worker. Such women sometimes appear incapable of running a home at all. It may be objected that this is not really a form of delinquent behaviour, but apart from the fact that serious neglect of children is an offence against the law, the woman of this kind is a potential delinquent. She is to be found, too, appearing in court on charges of obtaining goods by false pretences in a rather pathetically obvious manner. In many cases she is quite unable to resist the door-to-door salesman, and her household economy is always in a hopeless state. Quite frequently, such women are of low intelligence, and, perhaps to some degree as a result of childbearing and undernourishment, in poor health also.

We are well aware that there are also many neglectful fathers and husbands, but the position of mother in the home and family makes it a matter of greater concern when she fails in this way. Some women seem not so much incapable as overwhelmed by the demands of husband and family, and to have given up the struggle. Once again, it must be emphasized that every individual must be separately considered from the viewpoint of treatment, but the problems and their effects will appear similar in many respects in large numbers of families.

There is no use in pretending that it is easy for social workers to offer a ready-made solution to such women. Indeed, in our experience, if any help can be given it is frequently much better done by two workers if this is possible, of whom one should interview the mother and the other the father of the family. The matrimonial situation is often the best way of approach, and if this is attempted by one worker only it may be found that the making of useful relationships with both husband and wife is impossible because of their feelings of mutual suspicion and mistrust, and their frequent appeals to the social worker as an arbiter. Discussion of this situation may be found in *A Modern Approach to Marriage Counselling*[1].

Sometimes it is possible, especially with younger women, to make such an approach that the mother is able to look with the worker at the relationships existing in her own family. The possibility of ultimate help may be greater if the mother can do this usefully. In some cases, for example, she may become able to talk about some of the hitherto unexpressed feelings which have been producing worry and conflict in her mind. If the social worker can achieve a relationship within which this takes place, it may be that the woman can look at the good feelings she has as well as getting emotional relief in seeing that the bad feelings are accepted. She may come to experience less hopelessness, for instance, and draw from the relationship some confidence. Even a small amount of confidence can help a great deal.

If the case is treated as a marital one, perhaps with two social workers co-operating, the husband may be shown something of the part he is playing, or failing to play, in the complex pattern of family life and feeling. Even more may then be done to enable them both to look at their problems for themselves. The solutions they try to work out may not be those which the social worker would have chosen or suggested. The important thing is that they are attempting together to work towards some goal, even a limited one. All too often, without the help of someone else who can see a beginning of the process, they do not even visualize any way out of the practical and the emotional difficulties which they see all round them. Practical help in budgeting for the household, and in such matters as cooking and keeping the home clean, or taking up outside interests, may help at first, but such assistance or training must be combined with an attempt to give some insight and understanding, even at a simple level, if it is to be of lasting value.

We quoted at the beginning of this chapter the opinion of Bovet that the emotional difficulties of women frequently do not show themselves in openly delinquent behaviour, but are shown in family problems after marriage. This is true of the kind of women we have just been discussing, and when the social worker attempts to help such women the position of their children should especially be considered. The possibility of overt delinquency in the boys and of less obvious emotional problems in the girls is quite strong, and it is of importance that social workers in touch with such mothers should consider, at the earliest possible stage, seeking the opinion of the child guidance clinic workers as to whether their help may also be needed. It may not be easy to get co-operation in this from such families, but the attempt ought to be made. Environmental factors are also of great importance in homes of this kind, although re-housing may be extremely difficult and may raise as many problems as it solves.

So far we have discussed females in whom there has

not necessarily been any known delinquency of a more usual kind, such as stealing, in which direct comparison with males is possible. Not only is the number of women and girls who steal small as compared with men and boys, but they do not continue to offend. Over 80 per cent of females complete a period of probation without coming before the court again, as compared with 70 per cent of males. At the other extreme, only ten females were sentenced to corrective training or preventive detention in 1959, against a total of 617 males.

In this same year of 1959, there were 17,456 females found guilty of indictable offences. Of these, no fewer than 6,643 were charged with stealing from shops or stalls. 8,080 men appeared on this charge, out of a total of 135,744 who were dealt with for indictable offences. This means that 38 per cent of females were guilty of shoplifting, as against only 6 per cent of males.[40] The increasing number of shops which display goods of all kinds casually set out and with no apparent guard provide great temptations, but these are open to men also, so that even allowing for the fact that women are far more likely to go into these shops, the disparity of these figures is surprising.

There are, as is well known, women who are professional shoplifters, and these will adopt numerous ruses to carry on their stealing undetected. The problem which concerns the social worker more, and which seems to have grown more acute of recent years, is that of the 'respectable' woman who steals trifling articles when she has plenty of money with her. The experience of the authors regarding women who take things in this apparently purposeless way is that the majority of them have some form of emotional problem. With married women, the problem may also produce marital difficulties, either overt or, more usually, concealed, which raise emotional conflict.

Neustatter[41] suggests tentatively that there may be a compulsive element in such stealing, and that perhaps the acquisition satisfies some deep craving, for affection, attention, or sexual satisfaction, for example. It may, he says, 'be part of an hysterical make-up – the personality which cannot tolerate ordinary frustration . . .' Perhaps also there are organic factors present in such women which produce or add to the psychological ones.

Most courts use punitive methods when dealing with shoplifters, usually heavy fines, so that knowledge of deeper motives which would develop from prolonged contact is not easy to obtain. In addition, since this offence is not confined to any social class, and women from the so-called 'respectable' classes commit it, there is often a factor of social disgrace which in itself may produce severe emotional reactions. These add further confusion to the basic emotional stress.

Many explanations have been put forward for the fact that such a disproportionately large number of women steal in this way. It has been discovered that in many cases it occurs during the menstruation period. This would indicate some sexual basis; it is, for example, the time when some women are said unconsciously to feel most envious of men and resentful of them. Some probation officers have found that shoplifting also occurs, significantly, at the time of the menopause, and during the later stages of pregnancy. It may well be that the stealing is an expression of heightened emotional tension. We are not familiar with any valid statistics about these suggestions. The women referred to the social worker are in any case only a small minority of those found guilty, and probably a minority selected for the very reason that they are in some way out of the ordinary run of shoplifters, so that no effective generalizations are possible. We have only mentioned here some of the possibilities to have in mind, but we are sure that underlying many cases there is much emotional distress which may be relieved by the social worker's support and insight.

A short example may illustrate the kind of situation which at first appears baffling, and show how the feelings and motives grow much clearer if the social worker does not accept the merely surface suggestions offered. Mrs G was placed on probation for stealing from a shop some bars of chocolate valued in all at five shillings. She was about thirty-five, married for fifteen years, with a son at a boarding-school on a scholarship. Her husband was a managing clerk in a large firm of exporters earning about fourteen pounds a week, and they were buying their house.

At first Mrs G explained that they were hard-pressed for money, because of the expense of their son, and because her husband had to contribute to his widowed mother's upkeep. She told the probation officer that although she possessed a washing-machine, a television set, and other similar semi-luxuries (and her husband ran an old car), all these actually saved money. The reason she had taken the chocolate was 'a sudden temptation' and it was because she seldom had the money for small treats like chocolate.

The probation officer saw Mrs G fairly frequently at the office. It soon became clear that although she professed much love for her husband and her son, she dominated them entirely. The husband's great act of rebellion was to insist on sending his mother her allowance regularly. Mrs G talked continually about the uselessness of her husband: nothing he could do was right in her eyes.

After a time the probation officer began to understand some of Mrs G's need to dominate. At one interview especially, Mrs G told of her own childhood. Her father had died when she was very young – about three years old. It almost seemed that she blamed him for his death and was somehow determined to see her husband as a person who, like her father, was of no use to her. She had forced her son into a boarding-school against his wishes and those of his father, so as to be able to boast to her friends about him. He was unhappy there, but she refused to see this.

Although it was difficult at first, the probation officer was gradually able to put some of these feelings back to Mrs G in a way she could understand. After almost a year, she was beginning to tell the probation officer that she felt a bit worried because she lost her temper sometimes. This was received without criticism, and over a period Mrs G was more and more encouraged to talk of herself as a person who was not entirely good, but fallible like other people. With the probation officer she could express her bad feelings as well as her good ones. The relief of being treated exactly the same however she behaved, seemed to give her much emotional support. Her husband and son also noticed the difference, and one day all three of them engaged in the venture of decorating the house together. Moreover, they chose the colour-scheme together, instead of Mrs G dictating what she wanted.

She has never been in trouble since, and there is less tension at home. Mr G, though friendly to the probation officer, would not see her because, he said, he was not on probation, but he did have some interviews with a marriage counsellor which probably helped him also. The son, although he remained at his boarding-school, was allowed to choose his own career when he left school. In some ways he was a disturbed boy emotionally, but was able to become more confident when he was given more freedom of action and expression of opinion. He was greatly helped by psychiatric treatment.

In the case of Mrs G, therefore, it seems that the refusal of the probation officer to accept the explanation given at first, coupled with her ability to form a non-condemnatory relationship in which Mrs G could talk freely, gave some emotional relief which Mrs G had never before achieved. There are still problems and quarrels; Mrs G has certainly not become an angel of reason and amiability. But the development which has taken place seems to have been sufficient to help not only her but her husband and son also.

We shall mention only very briefly our fourth type of female delinquency. This is not because it is not important, but because we feel that it is unlikely that many social workers can successfully treat in the way we have described in this book, a woman who has taken up prostitution as a profession. Since the publication of the Wolfenden Report,[42] much attention has been directed towards the subject, and it is to be hoped that more useful research will be devoted to the psychology of the prostitute. The kind of girl who becomes promiscuous seems often to be one who feels deeply rejected by her family and by society at an early age. She presents a barrier of indifference to everything outside her private world. Obviously there are infinite variations in both motivation and object, but case-histories given in *Women of the Streets*[43] for example, indicate that prostitutes usually come from broken and unhappy families. It is better and more hopeful to attempt to recognize in young girls the signs which point towards promiscuity, to look at these with the girl, and try to help her to see at this early stage something of her feelings and underlying emotions.

It may be thought that the kinds of conduct which have been discussed in this chapter have been arbitrarily selected or superficially treated. Our principle, however, has been to show that although the delinquent and anti-social feelings of girls and women may take different forms of expression from those of their male counterparts, treatment by social worker is still dependent upon the same approach and upon the building-up of the same kind of relationship.

A final point which may be raised concerns the question as to whether a delinquent of one sex can be helped by a social worker of the opposite sex. In the Probation Service this is not generally permitted except with young boys, and it must be recognized that there are practical difficulties. Given the right circumstances, we feel that effective help can be given. This will often emerge in the sharing of a case between men and women social workers. It is also borne out by the success of the work undertaken, particularly in the fields of marriage counselling and mental health, where this question is not at issue.

XVI

Interviewing

In this chapter we shall draw together and make clearer some of the aspects of the method which we have so far discussed. The interview is the chief tool of the social worker in his approach to any client, and through this the personalities and the situations involved are made alive. By means of the interview everything which may be brought forward is discussed and talked about by both the social worker and the client. As one interview succeeds another, and the discussions continue, a deeper understanding may be achieved through the sharing of problems which becomes possible.

The term interview is used here in a much wider sense than is usual. It does not just mean that one person is being talked to by another, or judging another, or is even seeking information in some way. The overall object of the interview for the social worker is to make the kind of relationship with the client which has been discussed in earlier chapters.

It may be objected that both in interviewing and in the making of a relationship, the essential personal qualities required are such that the use of one particular method is not practical. This is not true, since a social worker can adapt a method to his own personality, and so not lose his individual approach. He can fit the ideas to his own way of interviewing, and not try to alter himself to the ideas.

The interview provides in general the opportunity for the interplay of feeling between the social worker and the client, and allows the latter to show his deeper needs. He will usually at first put himself forward either as the person he thinks he ought to be, or as the person he thinks the social worker wants him to be. It is essential for the worker to try to look with the delinquent at the sort of person he really is. This may itself result in the relief of tension, since he is talking to someone who is at least trying to see things his way.

In early interviews the social worker will need to make some assessment of the client and the situation. This should not be done too quickly, nor should the social worker get involved too deeply in any way at an early stage. If he does so, he may find it difficult to make a really objective approach at a later date either to the client or to his problems.

The immediate purpose of the interview is of much importance. This may be specific: for instance, to get the information for a report, or to see whether a delinquent is suitable for membership of a youth club. On the other hand, it may be more general: for example, an interview by a child care officer with a neglectful mother. In some cases, much of the attention must be directed to facts. If the interview is undertaken in order to present to a court a report on the social background of an offender, much of the substance will be factual, although not necessarily all. Furthermore, the report will be given to other people such as magistrates. It may be read in open court. In addition, it may not result in what the delinquent considers to be his own good – he may be sent to prison as a result of it. A report of this kind must be as objective as possible from the viewpoint of the social worker, who may be questioned by the court on the contents of the report which he presents. Often, however, there is no immediate purpose of this kind in the interview, so that it is very necessary for the social worker to keep well in mind his own aims and objectives.

We have in earlier chapters looked at the use of the interview in making the relationship between the worker and his client, and seen what some of the aims may be. The worker may be trying to get information of various kinds, to understand the client, to help the client to understand himself, to demonstrate his own concern and interest, and to help the client in his own efforts to establish some code of conduct which is possible for him. There are clearly other purposes which social workers will feel are suitable for their own particular work or personality, and what we suggest here is simply the outline of a method. But before going any further it is necessary to look at some practical points of importance to the social worker in his interviewing.

The actual setting will vary considerably. The interview with the delinquent is ideally carried out in the office of the social worker, but there will be a very large number of occasions on which this will not be possible. For example, many social workers have offices which for some reason are not suitable for this, perhaps because they are shared with several others or because of the probability of interruption, maybe at a critical point in the discussion. Sometimes the delinquent lives too far away from the office of the worker to make it practical for him to call there. He may be too young for such a journey or such a call to be desirable. For these and other reasons the best course may be impracticable. In such circumstances the social worker will have to make the best of what he has at his disposal, and try to see the client alone in a room at the client's home, or in some other place. The essential requirements are privacy and, as far as is possible, freedom from interruption. Cheerfulness and lack of formality can also help in many cases – we mentioned in Chapter XI the feelings that people may recall about the headmaster's study!

The advantages of using the office for the interview are of several kinds. Apart from privacy and freedom from interruption, there will normally be practical matters to be considered, such as the presence of a telephone, the availability of records, and possibly of secretarial help. Again, most social workers will perhaps feel more at ease in the surroundings to which they are accustomed, and although it may be said that it is better for the client to feel at home, in fact it is quite a useful aspect of the interview to notice how he reacts to another place outside his own home. It may indeed be easier for him to be able to lay aside for a time the associations which his own home holds for him.

Although the first meeting between social worker and delinquent may be in a setting not arranged by either, it is important for the worker to notice the initial reaction, manner, and attitude of the other. From the way he enters the room it may often be possible to observe whether he is relaxed or in a state of tension. His first words can be quite revealing, and the way in which he says them, coupled with his actual approach to the social worker, may help further to establish some idea of his feeling at that moment. It will at least provide a clue to the way in which he faces the situation.

At this first meeting, and indeed in subsequent meetings until a relationship has been established, both worker and delinquent are looking at each other and trying to 'size one another up'. The manner of the worker will be important to the client. Most social workers will show courtesy and respect towards their clients, even the least promising-looking, because this may be the first time that the client has been treated in this way. As we have seen, even when the worker feels the necessity to show anger and to warn the delinquent, this can be done without treating him as inferior. An old friend of the writers who helped many of the 'toughest' lads had a large house in which he put them up while they went out to work, until they could get on their feet and find lodgings for themselves. The first thing he ever said to each of them as he shook hands was 'In this house everyone is a gentleman until he is proved otherwise.' Many of them laughed at him, but even these came in time to understand that he meant that they would be treated as responsible and individual persons, often for the first time in their lives, and that they would be expected to treat others similarly. This may seem a simple and almost naïve approach, but it certainly worked, frequently with most unlikely material. In its way, it was a personal method of demonstrating concern and understanding for the needs of the delinquent.

Another important point when interviewing people who may be in a state of tension, defiance, or apathy, as so many delinquents are, is that if possible there should be some ease of manner on the part of the social worker. We have already shown that he may have a too-anxious approach on his side, but he must try to see what the first reaction of the client is to him. The early remarks of the worker should be as non-committal as possible, because the opening of an interview is sometimes its most critical phase. If then there is a relaxed appearance on the part of the social worker, this may communicate itself to the delinquent and make it easier for him to start where he feels it most important, and not where the worker suggests he starts. As we shall see, the matter of where the client begins the interview is also a very useful pointer as to what may lie behind his difficulties.

A matter worth attention is that of keeping clients waiting. If the delinquent has been waiting for some time in a room crowded with others who have been in trouble, apart from the obvious dangers of association he may come into the interviewing room in a frame of mind which the social worker is not easily able to appreciate. If possible, a system of appointments should be adopted.

The first interview with a delinquent may be the most important in many ways. If the delinquent decides that the social worker is not really interested in him, or is prejudiced against him, the likelihood of help being given is made more difficult. The people who come to social workers are often the very people who are most eager to seize the opportunity of saying that they are always misjudged and rejected. To avoid giving such an impression in the first interview is thus very necessary.

For this reason it is wise to start interviewing a delinquent with a remark such as 'Would you like to tell me about what's happened?' If this is done, his response can be taken up fairly easily, as this is an open question implying very little. If he says that he doesn't want to talk, the social worker can try to take up the reasons for this. On the other hand, if he asks what good it will do him, the worker can begin to talk about his own position and functions. In any case, this ought to be done at an early stage in the interview. Social workers are often inclined to assume that their clients know exactly what their particular duties and aims may be, only to find that many of those who are sent to them have little idea of these.

It is good practice therefore to get across to the delinquent a picture of where the social worker stands in the interview: to make it quite clear who the worker is, and what the possible objects of the interview or of the ultimate relationship may be, even though these may be limited at first.

As an example of this, a young woman of about twenty was sent to a hospital during a remand from a magistrates' court. She had been in trouble before and had an illegitimate child. Whilst she was at the hospital she was interviewed by an almoner, who found her very suspicious and uncommunicative. This is not unusual, and the almoner persevered. After seeing the girl twice she did not feel she was making much progress, and so the next time they met she opened with the remark, 'I wonder why you're so bothered about talking to me. I'm one of the almoners here, and my job is to help you while you're in here so that you can go out happier and look after yourself.' The girl was silent for a moment, then she said, 'Well, if you are one of the lady almoners, I'll talk to you, but I've had so many people worrying me, I don't know who they were, and I'm afraid of the reporters too.' The girl had been interviewed during the past two years by five different kinds of social worker, none of whom had made clear either their position or what they were trying to do. Moreover, the girl had been involved in a case which had been prominently reported in the local newspapers, and she was frightened of the probable renewed publicity which would accompany this fresh trouble. Fortunately, the almoner was able to give the girl some reassurance about her own position as a social worker, and to gain her confidence to some degree. As a result, much more help could be given to the girl when she reappeared in court after the remand hearing, and even her terror about 'the papers' was reduced.

In the Probation Service, particularly, it is important to deal quite clearly with these twin questions of aims and limits. If an inquiry for a court is undertaken, its objects ought to be explained to the delinquent as simply as possible. When a person is placed under supervision, the position of the probation officer, as distinct from the requirements of the probation order, ought to be dealt with, whether the delinquent accepts their implications or not. With young delinquents especially, the probation officer must try to make clear what his functions will be *vis à vis* the parents. In some cases the delinquent has no idea what the role of the probation officer may be. Sometimes the probation officer may assume that the reading over of the probation order and a sort of general knowledge of his work by the person under supervision is sufficient. Later events may prove however, that both the lad and his parents regard the probation officer's function quite differently from reality, and that each has a different conception of the officer's powers, responsibilities, and eagerness to help rather than to punish.

Experience will teach the social worker that many clients, if encouraged by suitable opening remarks, will begin at the point where they feel their problems are centred. The best answer to the question 'Where shall I begin?' is to say something like 'Where you feel you are most upset', or 'Tell me what you want to, in your own way'. A less suitable opening is for the worker to say 'What did you do this for?' It is very rarely that a delinquent really answers this, because it has so many possible angles – the practical, the emotional, the assumption that it was the client's fault, or even, if spoken in an exasperated way, the idea that the social worker is a judge or a parent with a small child. The social worker may have either or both of these feelings, but to show them at once in this way will seldom help.

Information will often be given almost unconsciously, without any questions being asked, provided that the social worker can sort it out from the other conversation. Direct advice and questioning are to be avoided, as a general rule, until a later stage of the relationship, unless circumstances make this unavoidable. Similarly, the social worker should keep before him the need to let the delinquent talk, and for himself to keep away from giving a lecture. There may be, as we have seen in earlier chapters, the need to have some control of the client's talk if this becomes an excessive outpouring of words. But one of the important things to learn about interviewing is to try not to hurry – to make another appointment rather than to have to rush through an interview – in spite of the fact that there may be what seem urgent pressures on both sides. If, therefore, the client wants to talk it is better to let him, within reason.

The differences in the interview situation are, of course, almost numberless. They will range from the obsessional talker to the client who has difficulty in talking at all. There is a great value in some silences, because they may help the client to collect his thoughts and as it were to nerve himself for his next remark. On the other hand, they may become too prolonged, and in this case may be resolved by a general remark from the social worker about the difficulty of talking about the things one feels most deeply, or, like the almoner in the earlier example, asking more directly if the client can say where the difficulty lies. There are, indeed, cases in which much has been accomplished because an understanding social worker was able to keep silent and allow the client the opportunity of simply sitting and sorting out his ideas with nobody to keep interrupting his thoughts. Such silences may become a sign that both are secure in the relationship.

We showed in earlier chapters that some of the feeling the delinquent displays in an interview will be irrational and that the social worker must allow for this. The worker should realize that even his personal appearance may strike some chord of like or dislike in the delinquent, of which neither may be aware. The feeling in the early interviews needs, therefore, to be handled carefully, but with increasing self-awareness on both sides the interview will become more of a consultation between people who can each contribute something of value.

An insidious danger to be guarded against is that a form of collusion may take place between social worker and client. One aspect of this has already been touched upon in Chapter IX, but it may occur in a less obvious way. It will sometimes happen that a social worker feels he is making a very good relationship with a client, when all that is happening is that both are tacitly avoiding the dangers of looking too deeply into the real problems. Perhaps the social worker may be a little frightened that if he tries to uncover the outer layers of the client's personality it will disturb or excite the client, and a hostile attitude will emerge. On the client's side, he may feel 'safe' with the social worker so long as the worker keeps the interviews on the surface. So long as the social worker realizes what is occurring, and consciously accepts the position for reasons which he feels to be good and sufficient, this situation may be the best for both. Where, however, it is an unconscious collusion, little work of a positive nature is accomplished. Such situations are those which should be discussed at case conferences or with experienced colleagues if possible.

This kind of interviewing can slip very easily into the situation where the worker and the client indulge in a form of mutual admiration, which may well result in dependence arising on both sides. It is evident that this is unlikely to result in helping the delinquent, and probably not the social worker either. The social worker of course must avoid seeking appreciation, however subtle the form in which it is offered. On the other hand, a reasonably friendly attitude in the developing relationship augurs well for future possibilities. The social worker must in fact try to achieve a friendly independence and guard against mutual dependence developing and stultifying the relationship for the purpose of real understanding.

It should hardly be necessary to emphasize again the difficulty of the social worker who has serious personal reactions to the particular delinquency with which he is confronted. In this the importance of self-awareness is clearly an essential consideration. The woman worker, for example, becoming too emotionally involved in the sexual adventures of the girls with whom she is dealing should do her best to look at the reasons for this, if she becomes aware of it.

Another more subtle occurrence in interviewing is a tendency to 'classify' delinquents almost on sight, or after one or two short interviews. There may be those clients whose needs are so clear that it is possible to say at once that this man is a psychopath, or that this woman is emotionally immature. It should however be done, if at all, with much caution, especially if subsequent treatment by interview is to be based on this diagnosis. It is better by far to assume that each person is an individual rather than a member of a typical class, whose reactions and emotional 'drives' can be accurately forecast and either dealt with or ignored.

Some interviewing, such as that carried out by a probation officer in regular meetings with those under his supervision, may be thought to be more difficult because the delinquent is under compulsion to come. Sometimes the officer can get over this by letting the compulsion slip into the background, and emphasizing the need of the delinquent to talk irrespective of the compulsory element. If this can be done, it is the best way, so long as the original hostility of the delinquent, if such hostility is present, is dealt with. If it is side-tracked by the effort of the worker to appear as a helping person, then the sort of collusion which we discussed earlier may arise.

Again, this forced interviewing may be put to the delinquent as a form of necessary discipline at first, in the hope that a better relationship will develop later in which he will himself be glad to meet the worker when the aspect of compulsion has diminished. 'Reporting to the probation officer', initially at any rate, may have an important part to play in the 'line-drawing' which has already been mentioned.

There is also another aspect. If it is possible to obtain through this 'reporting' some relationship of either a negative or a positive kind, at least this relationship is continued for a definite and regulated period. It has been remarked, for example, by a psychiatrist, that since his treatment of most patients is of a voluntary nature on their part, he has frequently lost contact with people whom he might have helped, whereas if there had been an element of compulsion this treatment might have continued with great benefit to the patient after the initial difficulties had been overcome.

There may enter into the relationship a question which has always been an accepted element in the consultations of the established professions with their clients or patients – that is, its confidential nature. Social workers must make it clear that their clients can talk and that nothing of what is said will be divulged to anyone else unless it is with the client's permission, or at the least with his knowledge. This may lead to difficulties where a delinquent or any other client confesses to some offence he has committed. Here the worker is forced into a situation where his duty as a professional person is in conflict with his duty as a citizen. We feel it impossible to lay down any rule for this situation, since the circumstances will vary so widely. It is suggested that the best course is to try to persuade the client to go to the police with the worker, or to allow the worker to inform them. In extreme cases, it may be necessary to tell the client quite definitely that the police or other authority are being informed. The social worker in such cases is in perhaps a somewhat similar position to the medical practitioner who is informed by a patient that he contemplates suicide.

In the same way that a medical practitioner will consult a specialist or a solicitor will approach a barrister, it is evident that the social worker must be prepared at a necessary stage in any relationship to consult other and more expert people. In this case, the confidence of the other person consulted should be a foregone conclusion. If social workers in this country are to be regarded as professional people, they must accept the responsibility in both the confidential and the consultative aspects of their work.

To summarize briefly, in this kind of interviewing the social worker is trying to establish with the client a relationship within which they can together look at the problems which the delinquent feels he can bring forward. These problems may not necessarily reach down to the roots of his personality, but they may not be so superficial as they seem at first. The worker will look beyond the words and phrases for feelings which may not easily be expressed, and will try to show them to the client. From the interviews he may get information of a practical kind which he may need to help the delinquent or for other purposes. By his manner and approach the social worker must express his real concern for and understanding of his client, and an acceptance of him, if not of his delinquency. Through the interviews some assessment of the delinquent and his real needs must also be sought, as well as some possible line of treatment to be put into operation, either in a practical way, or by a form of approach in subsequent interviews. There must be a knowledge of the feelings which arise in the interviews and of the manner in which they may be explained or at least shown to the delinquent. The aims and the limits of the work undertaken should be made clear. Finally, there should be no breach of confidence except with the permission or knowledge of the client, and then only to other people concerned in a serious way. It is of great importance for this to be as implicit in the relationship between social worker and client as it is in any other professional relationship.

XVII

Visiting the Home

Home visiting gives an opportunity to look at the emotional as well as the material situation of the delinquent. The cross-currents of feeling between members of the family are important, as are factors of health, intelligence, material environment, leisure pursuits, and the attitudes towards authority which the parents assume. They have all to be taken into account when the social worker visits a home.

Of all these factors, we have so far looked mainly at the feelings and significant elements which are not at once obvious. Although it is essential never to lose sight of the deeper meanings of behaviour and the clues to personality, it is also necessary to observe the material environment and what might be regarded as the surface picture as shown in the family circle. After all, most social workers are not concerned only with seriously disturbed people.

Whatever may be the actual occasion of a visit to the family of a delinquent, the social worker must initially be keenly aware of this material and largely surface element. It will, of course, inevitably shade into the deeper and the more personal. For instance, if we notice that there are several children sleeping in the same room as their parents we shall register as a fact that the home is overcrowded, but we shall keep in mind also that there may be effects on the personalities of all or some members of the family, contributing to their problems. In this chapter we shall look at some of the many pointers to family background and relationship which may be found by the trained person, and at some of their significance.

We have commented earlier on the 'cultures' of different neighbourhoods, and noticed that even in adjoining streets quite surprising differences are found. Perhaps the neighbourhood is a pleasant suburban estate, with well-kept gardens, and houses in good repair, so that the worker will expect to encounter a family in reasonable material circumstances, or at least trying to 'keep up appearances'. If the house visited is grossly neglected and stands out in startling contrast to these surroundings, then the visitor will feel (although he may later be shown to be wrong) that the family are not fitting in with their neighbourhood for some reason. He may also think that the children may be unacceptable to their neighbours, driven in on themselves, or forced to make friends elsewhere. This is a very considerable generalization, and it may turn out that the family is merely happy-go-lucky, refuses to conform to outward conventions and possesses a cheerful independence which is sometimes refreshing. It is certainly dangerous to generalize unless one is prepared to reconsider first impressions. However, it is fair to say that when confronted with this situation the first reaction might be that the family is at least somewhat isolated, if not actually ostracized.

The first observation, then, is of the district, the street, and the house. Impressions of these are important to the social worker because he will have to consider later how the delinquent and the family are influenced by them, and how they may be expected to react to them. It must be emphasized that here he must be careful to try to understand how the family themselves feel. For instance, if he is visiting a street crowded with children playing, mothers gossiping at front gates, with houses close together and in varying degrees of disrepair, he must try to set aside his own background if it differs from this. He must look through the eyes of his client, and realize that the person he is to see has probably spent all his life in this kind of world, and finds it friendly, cheerful, and kindly. The people who live here would miss the noise, the close human contacts, the day-to-day gossip, and even the quarrels and fights, if they were translated to the world in which the social worker himself may move.

When the social worker arrives at the house, the general condition will usually be fairly evident at once. He will, of course, notice whether any sort of pride seems to be taken in the appearance of the house and garden. This may enable him to make a rough-and-ready guess at the atmosphere of the home itself, since it provides some general indication of the front the family shows to the world.

The first contact with one of the family is of importance also. The social worker needs to state why he has come and who he is, but he must be sure that the person who answers the door is the right one to have this information, and is not perhaps a visiting neighbour.

A small pointer to the family attitude (or perhaps to its social traditions) may lie in the difference between an invitation to enter the home, and the expectation that the entire conversation is to be conducted on the doorstep.

Nowadays the social worker may find that the family

is sitting engrossed by the television. This situation may provide practical difficulties, but at least the family reaction is helpful in assessing its general attitude to the delinquent, the social worker, and to the television! It may show, for instance, whether the visit is regarded as being of importance. The social worker can also see which of the family is most concerned about the delinquent person who is the subject of the visit. It may indeed be useful in estimating a number of different family relationships. If, for example, mother suggests that he might like to see the delinquent in another room, or if father suggests that the set be switched off, the reaction of each of the family can be gauged. Even if the set remains switched on, and the family make the social worker feel as though he is an interloper who is hindering their enjoyment, this is of use in interpreting their general attitude. Where one of them is the subject of a serious charge and the social worker is a probation officer making an inquiry for a court, an attitude of indifference such as this is of considerable significance, and could reasonably be commented upon to the parents or the delinquent himself.

The question of the making of relationships, which dominates the process of treatment by social worker, is immediately important here. Whatever the actual purpose of the visit, some kind of relationship will be generated or developed. In some cases the social worker may think that no useful purpose is served by an attempt to see what kind of relationship is developing, nor how it progresses during what may be only a short visit. But nobody can tell what may be the future needs of the delinquent or the family, and it is always relevant to consider the nature of the relationship formed.

Once inside the home, the number of impressions which will crowd in upon the social worker is enormous, and it may be worth repeating the warning that these will affect him subjectively – his feelings are not necessarily very objective, especially if he is inexperienced. He may feel that the home has about it a cheerful casual atmosphere, and a lack of restraint of which he approves. On the other hand another social worker visiting the same place might equally well perceive feckless disregard for ordinary good manners, lack of control, and untidiness. This subjective element cannot be eliminated from social work, but it can be reduced if each worker tries to understand honestly something of his own prejudices and foibles.

The nature of the home itself is clearly the first point to be observed, and the homes visited by social workers are of infinite variety. It must not be assumed that the family which appears to be 'comfortably off', living in pleasant surroundings, is not in need of some help – an assumption all too often made by untrained persons. The special approach of the social worker may often reveal problems hitherto carefully concealed from the outside world. On the other hand, a family in crowded circumstances without much money may turn out to be happy and united, with children able to cope with life in their own way without serious difficulty. During the time the social worker is in the home he will be seeing in many small ways the sort of life which the delinquent person knows as his most intimate surroundings, and the influences which are being brought to bear on him. The actual physical conditions existing may be of importance to some social workers – for instance, if there is any question of placing a child with the family, obviously

considerations of hygiene and cleanliness may arise –
but in any case such physical conditions are indicative
of the attitude to life of the family. They should be considered as part of the background of the delinquent's
normal life.

There are, however, some practical considerations
which may arise. Where there is severe overcrowding it
may be that it is difficult to talk privately to anyone at all.
It is not really possible usefully to discuss her problems
with a delinquent mother when there is a ring of
inquisitive children standing round, or when they are
running in and out of the room. Although her reaction to
the situation is of much importance, it may be that the
only solution is for the visitor, once he has seen the home
and the people in it, and feels that he is in a position to
assess what he needs to get from the actual conditions, to
suggest an appointment at his office. Sometimes the
social worker may arrive when other people are present,
or during a meal, or even during a family crisis. He may
be offered a cup of tea, or even a share of the meal.
Many social workers feel that to have a cup of tea with
the family breaks the ice and establishes a friendly
basis. Here again something depends on the way in
which the offer is made, and the circumstances of the
visit. Some people see in such an offer a sort of attempt
to win over the social worker. There are others who
interpret such an invitation as indicative of hostility – as
an appeasement to someone who is unconsciously regarded with fear and suspicion. These varying aspects of
such a simple thing may serve as a caution to the inexperienced – or it may be that social workers have
become too deeply entangled with interpretation! Be
that as it may, our experience is that the great majority

of social workers accept the offer of a cup of tea quite readily.

The principles of interviewing remain the same whether people are seen in their own homes or in the office of the social worker. Similar reactions can therefore be noted and kept in mind, but there is the additional need to see the greater wealth of feeling shown between individuals. If the social worker is concerned with a particular member of the family who is delinquent, he must try to estimate some of those feelings and relationships already discussed in Chapter VII. It is relevant, for example, to try to assess who seems to have most control in the home. This is often seen fairly easily if there is more than one of the family present at any time during the visit, as this person will often tend to dominate the conversation. Where both parents are seen, it is naturally important to see whether one of them does in fact 'take charge', and how he or she does it. What has been said earlier about sensing the feelings towards the social worker must of course always be borne in mind.

If the visit is in the nature of an inquiry, it will provide a chance to see how each parent views the delinquent, or if the latter is an adult, how the other members of the family react. There should emerge from the interview some idea of the cross-feelings in the group: who seems to love whom: whether there is any resentment or friction apparent: something of the way the delinquent was seen when he was young. Some judgement should be made of individual personalities and their place in the delinquent's life. If there is a father, does he spend much time with the family and take a full share in its activities? Is he regular in his work, or does he change jobs frequently, with spells of unemployment?

Can father tell you much about the children, or does he leave this to mother? On the other hand, is mother really very concerned, or does she see herself in the role of a household drudge? Does she go out to work? If so, is it apparently necessary in order to balance the family budget, or is there some other reason? How is the money arranged in the family, and do all the members at work seem to make a contribution to its exchequer? How much are the others concerned about the delinquent member in whom the social worker is interested? Above all, what does the delinquent himself feel about these matters?

Such questions as these will not usually be asked in any definite form by the social worker, because if he asks too many questions he will get only superficial answers and these may not help him. What he must do is to try to cultivate the ability to see what lies behind a statement, and to allow people to talk as much as possible on their own. It is surprising how much more true and useful will be the information obtained with the very minimum of questioning.

When the social worker feels that he has achieved the object of his visit he must eventually take his leave. This, as in ending interviews, is not always easy to do at the right moment for himself, his client, and the family. For the social worker the proper time on an initial visit would seem to be when he feels he has begun to understand where the delinquent stands in his family and home environment, and when he has obtained sufficient factual information for his purpose. If he feels that a useful relationship has been started, he will be even more satisfied. But many difficulties may arise. For instance, the family may contain an over-anxious person desperately bidding for the support or goodwill of the social worker, or the latter himself may be over-anxious. Again, there may be considerable differences between the members of the family which have led during the visit to quarrelling and anger, so that the social worker may hesitate to leave without having made some attempt to pacify the situation. This is, perhaps, a symptom of his anxiety. In this kind of situation it is easy to prolong the visit to exhaustion point. It is also important in any visit, and especially when one is leaving, to have decided whether the association will be continuing either with the family or with the delinquent, or with both. Although much may be accomplished in a single visit, impressions on both sides will be confirmed or revised if contact is continued. Such a continuing relationship is the real basis of any attempt to help with the solution of the problems of the delinquent or of the family.

Where, therefore, one is prolonging the association, the matter of when to depart may not be so important, because any necessary work may be taken up at a later stage. The variety of situations and the numerous reasons for visiting make it impossible to lay down any rule. If there have been quarrels and differences either in the family or between them and the social worker during the visit, it may be better to point out where these diffi-culties lie, or to indicate possible courses, and to visit again at a later date. Perhaps by that time the family may have considered afresh what has happened and be more easily able to discuss the position, or the social worker himself may feel that he has misunderstood what he has seen. In any case, he may have had the chance to interview the delinquent subsequently away from the home, but fortified by the knowledge gained of the home and its emotional cross-currents and its whole atmosphere.

What has been said in this chapter may be applied to the visit of a social worker under most circumstances. It will be of more value to some than to others, partly because of the differing purpose of each visit, and partly because of the subjective nature of the whole approach. In the numerous cases where the social worker is trying to decide initially whether he shall work mainly with the delinquent, or mainly with the family, or perhaps whether he should work with one particular member such as mother or father, the considerations we have suggested here are of vital importance.

XVIII

Working with the Family

A home visit may be for purposes of investigation, for initiating a relationship or developing one; or for the purpose of giving direct help. The variations of the situation are very numerous and we can only speak in general terms.

The purpose of the visit will govern at least the opening phase, if not its whole course. There will, for instance, be a considerable difference in meaning both to the social worker and to the client and his family between the visit of a probation officer making an inquiry on behalf of a court, of a psychiatric social worker calling for the first time to make a social report for a psychiatrist, and a club leader trying to get the co-operation of parents in dealing with a difficult member of his group.

It is worth while considering here the meaning which the visit may have for the social worker and for the client and his family. The worker may come along feeling that he represents a helpful figure – a good person; he may assume that he will be received in this light. But this may not be the case, and he will have to sense the 'atmosphere' very carefully, especially during the earlier part of the visit.

Initially, the atmosphere may seem to be a happy one, but this may be only superficial. A warm welcome can cloak anxieties and resentment. The social worker may be seen as someone who will help in some way, or he may be seen as a threat, particularly to the 'respectable' family. In the case of the psychiatric social worker or the probation officer the hope of some assistance with a difficult member of the family is often present, together with a feeling that here is someone who will understand the family's fears, worry, or indignation. But these same workers can also represent a threat to the liberty of a family member and to the self-respect of them all. The very presence of the social worker may be seen as an attack on the security, privacy, and social standing of the family. Again, there may be a confused mixture of these feelings, so that there is something of both present. It is very important that these feelings should be perceived and understood by the visitor, and he must be careful that he does not so control the situation that 'everyone is happy'. If, for instance, there is some hostility, the social worker must decide whether to deal with this at once or take it up later, if there is likely to be a prolonged relationship. Much will depend upon his judgement of the intensity and importance to the relationship of the feelings involved, and also upon the time at his disposal.

Frequently the family will be trying to show what a 'nice' home they have. Sometimes they will try to impress upon the social worker how shocked they are at the behaviour of one of their number. On the other hand it may be that the reverse takes place: a protective attitude is shown towards the delinquent member by such remarks as 'He is easily led', or 'She has always been a very good girl before'. The classic and stereotyped phrase of the protective parent is 'He's always been a good boy at home'.

The actual interview situation in home visiting is not

very different from office interviewing. The social worker will seek both for information and for impressions of feeling and emotion. There are some social workers who feel some diffidence in making home visits at all, partly because of this double aim, and partly because they feel that it is difficult to make a meaningful relationship with a delinquent at the same time as trying to make one with his family. They feel that he may react with suspicion and mistrust to any contact with his family, so that a secure relationship between client and worker is jeopardized. This may well be true of disturbed people who have this insecure and jealous feeling as part of their disturbance. Certainly the social worker should at the first opportunity explain to the delinquent the precise reason for his contact with the family, and why it is necessary to visit the home. Occasionally it may be desirable to defer the visit until a sufficiently strong and positive relationship has developed between them so that the client may more easily accept this necessity. In some social work agencies the person concerned with interviewing the client does not visit the home, and this part of the procedure is taken over by another worker. On the other hand, in cases such as court inquiries by probation officers, the home visit is invariably regarded as essential, except, perhaps, where the person is in lodgings, or other special reasons apply.

Home visiting is normally an important part of treatment by social worker. Let us therefore look at some of the things he should be thinking about both before the visit and during its course. The visit to a home has a direct connection with the treatment of the delinquent person. We are mainly concerned with the family and its complex emotional situations as they affect him, not so much with its economic position, though this must also be borne in mind. It may be that the result of the visit will leave the family and the social worker with many other problems. For instance, the latter may be faced with a decision as to whether he must work with the parents rather than with the delinquent. It may be that he has become convinced that such serious problems exist in the environment that it would be impossible to undertake work at all with the delinquent himself and have any hope of success. This will lead to consideration about the advisability of removal altogether from the environment; or if this is impossible, to see whether the environment can be changed in some useful way. If this looks desirable and is possible, much thought will then have to be given to the best way of achieving it, bearing in mind the reactions that such change will have on all concerned – not merely on the delinquent person alone. It may be objected by some workers that the client alone should be taken into consideration, but we hold that the interplay of family relationships in the future must also be taken into account. If the delinquent is to return at some future time to this environment, as is usually envisaged, then the effects of his absence not only upon him but upon the other persons who are directly concerned should be a factor of some weight, as should the possibility of continued contact of a supportive nature between the social worker and the family during such an absence.

Let us look at an example where some of the points raised may be seen more clearly. A clergyman became aware that one of the girls in his Sunday school who was about thirteen years of age had recently become listless and anxious. The mother eventually took the girl to him because she had stayed out very late on several nights, and the mother was worried. He called at the home and found that the situation was somewhat out of the ordinary. The home consisted of the lower part of an old house. There were three rooms and a small kitchen: the family shared a bathroom with another family in the house. Father was a long-distance lorry driver, and mother had a part-time job as a cleaner. There was a son of eighteen who had just been called up for military service. Until he left, the girl slept in the same room as her parents with a screen around her bed. Father was often away at nights driving, and on such occasions she used to sleep with her mother. Now she had taken over her brother's room but still went into mother's bed when father was away.

The clergyman did not talk to the father, but he realized that from the girl's point of view this arrangement was far from ideal. Mother spoke well of the father, painting the picture of a good man who gave her the housekeeping money regularly, seldom went out except to work, and was good to his daughter. But the parson decided to enlist the help of a local woman social worker, who called at the home and soon formed a friendly relationship with the mother and daughter. This worker, however, was never allowed into the home when the father was there, because 'he was tired' or 'he had only just got in from work', or upon other pretexts. She soon realized that the mother was leaning heavily on her daughter – her emotions were directed so much to the girl that the latter was feeling worried and disturbed. The social worker knew that the girl was bearing much of her mother's anxiety and insecurity. In a deeper sense too there was probably an additional feeling, perhaps only half-conscious, of fear about replacing her father in some way with her mother.

From patient and understanding discussion it became clear that the underlying cause of mother's worry was anxiety about her husband. He had for some time been acting strangely. When he was at home he refused to go out at all, and would sit for hours staring at the fire. He became angry very easily and often refused to eat. He declared that all his workmates hated him because he was superior to them intellectually.

The social worker was alarmed by these symptoms, and felt that she ought to convey to the mother some of their possible import of mental illness, although she must not communicate her alarm. It happened that the girl caught a bad cold, and the social worker was able to suggest that the doctor ought to be called in. When this had been arranged, she was able to encourage the mother to mention to the doctor a little of her anxieties – at the same time she herself was able with mother's permission to see the doctor herself and explain more directly what she feared. In a short time the father entered a mental hospital and was later discharged, having much improved under treatment. During the period of his absence and after his return the family situation became less tense. The same worker kept in touch with the home, and was able to help all the family by her insight and the relationship which she was able to develop over an extended period.

In this case visiting the home was an essential part of the whole scheme of the work undertaken. It would have been difficult if not impossible to have accomplished what was done simply by office interviews. Initially, the social worker had only the details of the situation given her by the clergyman, and she felt that interviews at her office would not suffice. On the initial visit she was able to make a sufficiently good relationship with the mother to become accepted as a helpful figure, and was soon realizing that the girl's troubles about which the original contact was made were not the main factors in the problem. The emotional situation between members of the family had reached a stage where it was affecting them all to a serious degree, but none of them could appreciate the reasons, much less seek any easing of the tension. On her second visit she had to decide whether she could work with the girl or the mother or both. She had to set up some aim and work to it. In the event she decided to try to continue with both mother and daughter, and in fact it would have been difficult to work with either alone, still less with the father. The change of environment brought about for one member by the father's entry into hospital showed the way to some solution of the problem, although there will always remain some legacy of it. The position might have become much graver, with the probability of violence, but for the perceptiveness of the clergyman and the visiting of the social worker over a long period. It is probable that the girl herself would have drifted into some form of delinquent behaviour had the situation continued, or she would at least have been brought before a court as beyond the control of her parents.

The need for considering both the actual conditions in the home and the emotional feelings between the different members of the family is clearly brought out here. It was evident that the home had been crowded, but with the departure of the brother for his National

Service the untrained person might perhaps be forgiven for thinking the difficulties solved. She would not realize the burden upon the girl of her mother's emotional dependence, and in addition her real, although unconscious, anxiety about replacing her father in the bed when he was away. Although the social worker did not in fact try to deal with these unconscious feelings, she was able to recognize at least the probability of their existence and to understand that in a confused way the girl might have deep sexual fears about sleeping with mother. It is likely that in her talks with the girl she was able to convey her understanding of these problems without the need for deep discussion of them. This in itself would have been of much help to the girl and would enable her to express feelings which she could not even have hinted at in talking to her parents.

Apart from the girl, the social worker also realized the rift in the marriage situation. Before she could look at this with the mother it required a very positive relationship between them, and mother certainly could not express her real feelings about her husband until this had been achieved. Until she could feel secure in her relationship with the social worker the mother had to present her husband as a perfect father and husband. Once again, there was no need to go deeply into the mother's feelings about this – the sympathetic acceptance of them by the worker was enough at that time.

It may also be noticed that the social worker was able to recognize that the father's behaviour might be evidence of serious mental illness. It is interesting that she did not actually see the man at all until after he had returned home from hospital on leave, although he was in many ways the central figure. On the other hand, such detection of symptoms can be attempted only by very experienced people. In this case may be seen a combination of what might be called the 'environmental' and 'relationship' aspects of the social worker's treatment: alteration in some way of the environment, and the continuation of help of a supportive kind, which is carried out through the making of a good relationship. Even after the father had gone to hospital – which affected all the family individually and as a unit – all three of them continued to be interviewed and treated by different people who tried in varying ways to talk with them about their problems and help each to come to terms with their difficulties. In the case of the father, this was done by the psychiatrist in a hospital; the girl and her mother were assisted by social workers in another although equally important way.

A final point worthy of note is that the social worker realized that although the decision regarding the removal of father from home was not in her hands, it would affect all the other members of the family materially and psychologically. These effects were carefully considered, and the material aid was available in the form of helping mother to find work. This seemed to assist her to a position where she was able to lean less heavily on her daughter, although at first there was a heightening of her anxious worry, which was probably due to a feeling of guilt that she was in some way responsible for her husband's condition. Probably also the fact of being able to unburden herself to the social worker relieved her of the necessity of doing this to the daughter. The girl herself continued to occupy her brother's room, and here again the social worker was able to suggest to mother that she should discontinue the habit of sleeping with her daughter.

In this case perhaps we can see illustrated the three aspects mentioned in Chapter IV. The girl was certainly a potential delinquent, and the method applied showed first of all the use of change in her environment by removing the father. Next, there was readjustment of her own attitude to her environment. Finally, material provision was made – in a broad sense by the provision of the social worker as a person to whom she could talk, and in a narrow sense by direct assistance in helping mother into work so that the girl could continue to live in a reasonable manner. The need for these things to be recognized, distinguished, and considered in relation to each other is just as great in dealing with a case by visiting the home as in office interviewing. Observation of all the factors, both superficial and emotional, and ability to select and deal with them is the beginning of professional skill.

XIX

Recording, Assessing and Understanding

Much of this book has been spent in examining the impact of the social worker upon the delinquent and upon the delinquent's family. What happens when social worker and delinquent are actually face-to-face is very important, but just as important are the feelings about the relationship which continue between their meetings. Sir Basil Henriques, the distinguished juvenile court magistrate, wrote that in his view the effect a probation officer could have upon a delinquent must be limited because the actual time they spend together is such a tiny proportion of the delinquent's life.[44] This may be extended to include other social workers. What Sir Basil did not give full weight to, however, was that the time between meetings in a relationship of any depth can be of great value to the delinquent and also to the worker. Such a relationship deepens and develops between meetings.

Feelings are not limited by space, as is speech. Feelings between people can continue even though they are separated. Thus feelings may exist between social worker and delinquent even when they are apart. But feelings need time to develop. The relationship engendered by ten weekly meetings each of thirty minutes' duration is very different from that which might arise from one interview lasting five hours.

In the preceding chapters we have seen what kind

of feelings delinquent and social worker are likely to bring into their relationship, and how these might develop and be used in a positive way. We can now look at practical methods by which the worker may try to understand more clearly what is going on emotionally between himself and his client. It is possible for him to use constructively the proportionately long intervals between the meetings to deepen and enrich his understanding of the situation.

Recording is a major means of doing this, although the keeping of records by social workers about cases has other purposes also. It has for instance, an administrative function. Originally, the introduction of recording into social work was an attempt to ensure that the purposes of the social work agency were being properly fulfilled, and that the needs of people were being met in accordance with the policy of the agency. Not only was the record a statement of what the individual social worker had done, but it also extended and supported the social worker's recollection of his client. In this way the social worker could more easily understand what had happened between the client and himself. In addition, the records provided a means whereby his work could be checked and supervised. These administrative considerations are still relevant.

Of all social work agencies, whether statutory or voluntary, the Probation Service has one of the most highly developed systems of record-keeping. Probation records serve not only administrative requirements but research requirements too. However, in this book we are not concerned with these aspects other than to notice them. Our concern is with record-keeping as a means of understanding and following the development of the client–social worker relationship. This particular function of recording has grown as the aims of social work have been extended. It is still increasing in importance. We would go so far as to say that anybody who attempts work with delinquents in the open must try to keep some form of record, for this purpose if for no other.

As we have shown already, intuitive responses to people may be sufficient in ordinary life, but more than intuition is required from the practising social worker. The keeping of records is a means whereby he can attempt to clarify the situation between himself and the delinquent. It is a means whereby he can see the relationship in some sort of perspective and so use it constructively. He must try through his records to assess what has gone on, and to analyse the stages in the development of the relationship. By asking himself various questions, he will make his whole task easier. How does he see the delinquent? How does the delinquent see him? What does the offence mean to the delinquent? What does it mean to the worker? What does the client feel about his parents, wife, children, as the case may be? What does the worker feel about them? What are their reactions to the worker, and what function do they seem to think he fulfils? Thinking about these questions and answers and objectifying thought in a written record serves to focus attention and bring understanding to a conscious level.

Sometimes, particularly during his training, a social worker can be helped if he writes down a detailed description of what went on during an interview with a delinquent. This form of recording is known as 'process' recording. At the most elementary level, it helps the social worker to develop his perception of those intangible factors of posture, attitude and speech which are of such importance in understanding a person. The practising social worker will rarely have time for such lengthy methods. He will have to keep his records brief and concise if he is to cope with his case-load and keep abreast of his recording.

The keeping of really useful records requires experience, but nevertheless there is much that the beginner can learn in a short time. It is worth remarking first of all that a social work record must include some account both of fact and of feeling. Factual details will include the names and ages of the client and the members of his family, his address, his school, his educational standard, his health and employment record, the nature of his dwelling and its neighbourhood, his current offence and its circumstances together with his previous offences, if any. The feelings recorded will be principally those within the delinquent himself, in his family, and within the relationship between the delinquent and the social worker.

One method of recording provides for fact and feeling to be separated. Using this method, there would be a record of factual matters at the beginning, followed by a day-to-day account of meetings and contacts with the delinquent, and changes in his circumstances. Alongside this would be an assessment, at quarterly intervals or less, which would analyse the quality, direction and development of the feelings within the delinquent himself and in his family and, even more important, of the feelings between the delinquent and the social worker. A less rigid view is to recognize the difference between the recording of fact and of feeling but not to separate them entirely. The amalgam of fact and feeling which makes up the ideal record is subtle and elusive and can come only with experience.

The record will reflect to some extent the personality of the social worker himself and, consequently, complete standardization is difficult and undesirable. The record is not a showpiece, nor a justification or defence of the social worker's activities. A good record will usually show initial ideas, mistakes, revisions of opinion and even downright bewilderment. Orderliness and neatness are important, but it must be remembered that the record is a tool of the individual social worker and should not normally look so perfect as to indicate that it is seldom used. The trouble is that since professional social workers usually are required to keep records, many of them regard the task as a duty only. When recording comes to be seen as useful to oneself as well as to superiors and to succeeding colleagues, a decisive advance in professional development has been made.

Although such constructive record-keeping is helpful, there comes a time in some cases when the learner in social work is at a loss. His work with the delinquent seems to be leading nowhere. He may have rapidly formed what appeared to be a good relationship, but now he can go no further forward. Each interview seems to be only a sterile covering of ground already explored. Alternatively, a relationship has never developed. Despite every attempt, he encounters only missed appointments or sulky silence. Again, there are frequently factors in a developing relationship which are hard to understand. The delinquent and his parents perhaps are most friendly and superficially co-operative, yet real feelings are never shown. At another time the social worker may feel that a certain approach or course of conduct must be a good one, but still he may wonder if he is really being objective. For example, he may decide not to meet the father of a delinquent. In coming to this decision, he may wonder whether this represents an objective appraisal of the needs of the case, an antipathy towards the father, or even some fear. Situations such as these, and many similar ones, can be helped by what has come to be known as 'casework supervision'.

'Casework supervision' is an American term which may not always convey its real meaning. The word supervision is the bugbear. In practice it is a relationship between the social worker and a person more experienced in such work. It is intended to be a helping process and not an inquisitorial one. The main purpose is to help the social worker towards a deeper understanding of his client and of the relationship between them. Casework supervision in this form can be helpful for experienced social workers as well as for beginners, although for the latter it is particularly necessary. Teaching people to treat delinquency in the open is not a simple matter of imparting facts. Lectures and reading are valuable, but both have their limitations. What the individual social worker needs to acquire is an understanding of what goes on between himself and his client. He and his client are unique and so the relationship they form is unique. The best way for someone to learn to understand a unique relationship is to discuss it with a more skilled social worker. Side by side the two can sit down and draw out the tangled skeins, look at the feelings involved, and discuss aims and possibilities for the future.

It is within a good relationship with a skilled and experienced colleague that the social worker in training can be helped towards a knowledge of the unconscious feelings he may be bringing into a relationship. There are the likes and dislikes, the prejudices, or the unconscious attitudes towards people and situations. Someone not immediately involved in a relationship can see these where the learner himself may not. How the awareness of these feelings is brought to the consciousness of the learner is another matter. Casework supervision is a skilled process and we are only touching upon the fringe of it. It will be apparent from what has gone before that it is better for the social worker in training to be helped to discover for himself his hidden feelings than to have them pointed out to him. If he has to be directly told, then this needs preparation and should not be done suddenly or thoughtlessly.

Although the relationship involved in casework supervision may assist the social worker in training to understand himself in relation to his client, it is not intended as a means of personal therapy. The experienced colleague would normally not go so far as to give help to the social worker in his personal emotional problems. He must be careful, indeed, that the relationship does not drift into a therapeutic one. Both participants are wise if they keep their discussion centred upon actual cases and the feelings arising from the cases.

Casework supervision has been seen by some as a means for developing in the beginner maturity in the emotional sense, as the social worker himself may sometimes hope to do in his work with his clients. This may be a possibility when a highly-skilled 'supervisor' is training students, but we are not here concerned with it. Widening of experience and ability in social work naturally involves some growth or change, however small, in the personality. This is inevitable where a person is trying to learn to use his personality in a conscious attempt to effect change in others. But in the type of work we are discussing, this growth or change comes naturally and is not deliberately brought about by the casework supervisor.

If the casework supervision relationship cannot be therapeutic, it may be supportive. The social worker with delinquents is in continual contact with the maladjusted, the unstable, the socially disorientated, the mentally ill, the deprived, the distressed, and the depraved. Close day-to-day contact like this may sometimes lead to anxiety in him, however experienced he is. This may be immediately obvious and directly expressed, or it may appear outwardly as irritability, tiredness, impatience, and in other ways. It has been found that an experienced colleague in situations like this can be of considerable help, especially if a supervision relationship has been developed of mutual confidence. The supervisor – if such we must call him – being not immediately emotionally involved, can act as a channel for some of the social worker's anxiety. Needless to say, he will not advise or direct, but give sympathetic understanding to the social worker in looking at the latter's feelings in the case.

In a social work organization which possesses an administrative hierarchy, the senior worker may combine casework supervision with administration. This has its dangers as well as its advantages. The advantages of close contact with a skilled and experienced senior have been mentioned already. But the senior himself must be careful of two things in particular. First of all, his administrative function should not conflict with his other function of offering casework supervision. Secondly, he should not make his colleague either over-dependent or, conversely, antagonistic enough to resent the offer of help. The first contingency is particularly difficult, but nevertheless must be overcome, for if the senior is seen only as an inspector or as a detector of deficiencies or mistakes, the mutual confidence will not be there. Just as a condemning attitude in the social worker makes the delinquent defensive in his attitudes, so too does it in the relationship between the less experienced social worker and his senior. The senior will normally have to see by inspection that the administrative requirements of the agency are being met, but he must do what he can to ensure that this is seen as a different function from casework supervision. The avoidance of over-dependence and over-individualism too is difficult. A middle course should be steered, but it will be different for each individual.

There will be beginners in social work with delinquents who have no senior to consult. Education welfare officers, approved school welfare officers, and N.S.P.C.C. inspectors, for example, may be in this situation. If they have a more experienced colleague with whom they can occasionally discuss cases, their position will be more tolerable. Complete isolation undoubtedly can militate against the development of really effective work. Here case-conferences could be the answer. If social workers – especially beginners – who are isolated could regularly, even if infrequently, meet each other to discuss a case, the help given would be appreciable. The case-conference method of learning and support is workable on different levels according to the training and aims of the social workers concerned. If a skilled and experienced social worker is available to lead the discussion, so much the better. One disadvantage when operated among colleagues and among kindred workers is that it may expose the more sensitive to public criticism and comment which they feel they cannot face. It may sometimes cause the social worker who uses what he thinks is an older and simpler technique to feel disturbed by an approach that is apparently more advanced. This feeling is a symptom of the rapid strides social work technique has taken and, for the time being, it may be important to ensure that participants in case-conferences are working at something like the same level.

Conclusion

Western society today appears to have lost some of the spiritual inspiration it once possessed. There seem to be no adequate goals other than material ones. No rational explanation for existence is accepted which satisfies a majority of people. In this situation, the demands of the community are emphasized. The individual cannot be allowed free expression of his personality if this expression conflicts directly with the security of the community he lives in. On the other hand, the free society must tolerate some deviant behaviour, since to repress it totally would be the negation of freedom.

This dilemma is a very real one. There are strong pressures within our society towards the acceptance of the free expression of individual personality; at the same time, there are equally strong movements towards the extension of various forms of community control. In the field of delinquency, there is pressure to reduce the punitive element, and this implies increased acceptance of individual responsibility. Coexistent with this is the opposite demand for more regulation and control of the individual, which tends to diminish the area of personal responsibility. The situation is made more obscure by the widespread belief that the explanation of delinquency in terms of personality removes in some way the direct responsibility of the individual for his actions.

It is here that the social worker can function helpfully. In one sense, he is the interpreter of society to the individual, helping the delinquent to see the necessity to adjust to society's demands, and helping him to attempt this adjustment. Furthermore, he encourages the delinquent to accept responsibility for his actions and not to seek to avoid the consequences. In another sense, he is the interpreter of the delinquent individual to society, helping to temper the demands of society to the capacity of the delinquent.

Much of this can be attempted, as we have shown in this book, by assisting the delinquent to understand his feelings about relationships with others. This often requires the development of a special kind of relationship with him, and sometimes with members of his family. In the relationship with the delinquent, concern for him as an individual is vitally important; but, while he is 'accepted', his delinquent behaviour is not. The aim of the relationship with members of the family is to help to complete, in a manner beneficial to the delinquent, the pattern of family feeling.

The process is not one of repression but of growth. It involves help from the social worker, however little it may seem, in the removal of obstacles which prevent the delinquent from realizing his best self. There is in each one of us a duality of good and bad feeling, and so often the bad overlays the good and stifles it. The methods we suggest are not a 'putting in' of goodness, but rather an attempt to help in drawing the good feelings out. We have said little of spiritual matters, being unqualified to do so, but it is perhaps in this light that our approach will be acceptable from the orthodox religious standpoint.

If we have unwittingly implied that the work of helping delinquents is easy, we should like to correct this.

CONCLUSION

Although immensely rewarding and worthwhile, the task is difficult and sometimes disheartening. We are very conscious that the social worker functions within a social setting over which he has little control and in which many of the forces and pressures are little understood. He works too amidst great and uncharted seas of human feeling, their extent unknown and their depths unplumbed. It is these reflections which render the social worker humble, and it is a spirit of humility which we commend to him in concluding this book.

Bibliography

1. W. L. HERBERT & F. V. JARVIS. *A Modern Approach to Marriage Counselling.* Methuen, 1959.
2. J. F. S. KING (ed.). *The Probation Service.* Butterworth, 1958.
3. C. BURT. *The Young Delinquent.* University of London Press, 1952.
4. W. HEALY & A. BRONNER. *New Light on Delinquency and its Treatment.* New Haven, 1936.
5. C. SHAW & H. McKAY. *Juvenile Delinquency and Urban Areas.* University of Chicago Press, 1942.
6. T. FERGUSON. *The Young Delinquent in his Social Setting.* Oxford University Press, 1952.
7. J. B. MAYS. *Growing Up in the City.* University Press of Liverpool, 1954.
8. T. P. MORRIS. *The Criminal Area.* Routledge & Kegan Paul, 1958.
9. A. K. COHEN. *Delinquent Boys: The Culture of the Gang.* Routledge & Kegan Paul, 1955.
10. W. J. H. SPROTT (ed.). *Social Background of Delinquency.* University of Nottingham (mimeograph), 1954.
11. L. BOVET. *Psychiatric Aspects of Juvenile Delinquency.* W. H. O., 1951.
12. D. H. STOTT. *Saving Children from Delinquency.* University of London Press, 1952.
13. D. H. STOTT. *Unsettled Children and Their Families.* University of London Press, 1956.

14. J. Bowlby. *Forty-Four Juvenile Thieves.* Bailliere Tindall & Cox, 1946.
15. J. Bowlby. *Child Care and the Growth of Love.* Pelican Books, 1953.
16. W. F. Roper. *A Comparative Survey of the Wakefield Prison Population in 1948 and 1949.* Brit. J. of Delinquency, I, 4, April, 1951.
17. S. & E. Glueck. *Unravelling Juvenile Delinquency.* Harvard University Press, 1952.
18. S. & E. Glueck. *Predicting Delinquency and Crime.* Harvard University Press, 1959.
19. G. Hamilton. *Theory and Practice of Social Casework* (2nd ed.). Columbia University Press, 1952.
20. H. Perlman. *Social Casework – A Problem-Solving Process.* University of Chicago Press, 1957.
21. N. East (ed.). *The Roots of Crime.* (Chap. by P. D. Scott). Butterworth, 1954.
22. M. Grünhut. *Juvenile Offenders Before the Court.* Clarendon Press, 1956.
23. S. Freud. *The Question of Lay Analysis.* Imago, 1947.
24. A. Adler. *What Life Should Mean to You.* Allen & Unwin, 1931.
25. J. Jacobi (ed.). *Psychological Reflections: An Anthology of C. G. Jung.* Routledge & Kegan Paul, 1953.
26. T. A. Ratcliffe. *The Development of Personality.* Nat. Marriage Guidance Council, 1959.
27. R. G. Andry. *Delinquency and Parental Pathology.* Methuen, 1960.
28. *Report on the 15–18 Group.* H.M.S.O. (Crowther Report), 1960.
29. B. Wootton. *Social Science and Social Pathology.* Allen & Unwin, 1959.

30. A. AICHORN. *Wayward Youth*. Putnam, London, 1936.
31. M. BURN. *Mr Lyward's Answer*. Hamish Hamilton, 1955.
32. C. MORRIS (ed.). *Social Casework in Britain* (Chap. by W. G. Minn). Faber, 1955.
33. D. H. STOTT. *The Bristol Social Adjustment Guides*. University of London Press.
34. *School and Social Maladjustment of Youth*. Unesco, 1960.
35. E. GLOVER. *Roots of Crime*. Imago, 1960.
36. P. D. SCOTT. *Gangs and Delinquent Groups in London*. Brit. J. of Delinquency, VIII, 1, July, 1956.
37. J. RICH. *Types of Stealing*. Lancet, I, 496, 1956.
38. T. C. N. GIBBENS. *Car Thieves*. Brit. J. of Delinquency, VIII, 2, 1957.
39. British Journal of Delinquency, October, 1959.
40. *Criminal Statistics*, 1959. H.M.S.O. Cmnd. 1100.
41. W. L. NEUSTATTER. *Psychological Disorder and Crime*. Chris. Johnson, 1953.
42. *Report of the Committee on Homosexual Offences and Prostitution*. H.M.S.O. Cmnd. 247, 1957.
43. C. H. ROLPH (ed.). *Women of the Streets*. Secker & Warburg, 1955.
44. B. L. Q. HENRIQUES. *Indiscretions of a Magistrate*. Geo. G. Harrap, 1950.

Further Recommended Reading

General :

H. JONES. *Crime and the Penal System.* University Tutorial Press, 1957. A helpful and readable criminological textbook.

J. A. F. WATSON. *The Child and the Magistrate.* Jonothan Cape, 1942. An excellent description of the work of the Juvenile Courts.

J. D. W. PEARCE. *Juvenile Delinquency.* Cassell, 1952. A textbook on the medical aspects of juvenile delinquency.

K. FRIEDLANDER. *Psycho-analytic Approach to Juvenile Delinquency.* Routledge & Kegan Paul, 1947. A controversial but interesting interpretation of juvenile delinquency from the Freudian standpoint.

C. M. FLEMING. *Adolescence – Its Social Psychology.* Routledge & Kegan Paul, 1948 (6th imp. 1959). A study of the adolescent of considerable importance to the teacher, with special reference to the therapeutic effects of group membership and family acceptance.

The Social Services :

P. HALL. *The Social Services of Modern England.* Routledge & Kegan Paul, (2nd ed.) 1959. The standard comprehensive survey of the social services.

F. V. JARVIS. *The Social Services and the Marriage Counsellor.* National Marriage Guidance Council, 1959. A brief survey of the English social services.

The Probation Service:

J. F. S. KING. *The Probation Service.* Butterworth, 1958. This book, referred to in the text, is invaluable to all students.

H. H. COOPER. *Probation.* Shaw and Sons, 1949. The various Acts of Parliament, Regulations and Circulars relating to probation in England and Wales.

A. C. L. MORRISON. *Notes on the Law and its Administration in relation to the Work of Probation Officers.* Home Office, 1958. A summary of the legal framework in which the probation officer works.

Probation and Related Measures. United Nations, 1951. An exposition of the use of probation throughout the world.

Reports:

Report of the Committee on Children and Young Persons. H.M.S.O. Cmnd. 1191, 1960. Includes a helpful survey of the whole field of legal provision for young delinquents.

Mental Health at Home and Abroad (Chap. by P. D. Scott on the psychopath). Nat. Assoc. of Mental Health, 1960.

Home Office Research Unit: Delinquent Generations. H.M.S.O., 1960.

For Product Safety Concerns and Information please contact our EU
representative GPSR@taylorandfrancis.com
Taylor & Francis Verlag GmbH, Kaufingerstraße 24, 80331 München, Germany